Reaching 4 Europes

Stephen McQuoid

Reaching 4 Europes

Stephen McQuoid

GLO PUBLISHING

Published by GLO Publishing
78 Muir Street, Motherwell, ML1 1BN
www.glo-europe.org

Printed in Scotland

Cover design by Mark Shufflebottom

Other books by Stephen McQuoid

A New Kind of Living

A Guide to God's Family

And is it True?

Sharing the Good News in C21

The Beginner's Guide to Expository Preaching

Reaching Four Europes

FOREWORD

I count it a real privilege to write this foreword for my friend and colleague Stephen McQuoid's sixth book. God has gifted Stephen with the ability to write concise and helpful books on a range of topics involving mission and discipleship. This latest book addresses the present challenge of reaching Europe for Christ. His analysis and insight into how we have arrived at our present state of thinking in Europe is brilliant. We do need to understand the mindset of Europeans in order to effectively reach them with the Gospel.

For over thirty years, I have travelled throughout Europe with GLO Mission Teams. Europe is certainly a tough mission field and I would consider this book to be a tremendous tool in seeking to reach Europeans for Christ.

I would strongly recommend all those who are serious about evangelism in Europe to prepare themselves for an involvement in mission by reading this book. The book not only provides a concise analysis of European history but gives helpful guidance on how to communicate the absolute truth of the Gospel.

I know that I can express the appreciation of all the GLO European Committee in supporting Stephen in the publication of this exciting and challenging book.

John Speirs
GLO European Co-ordinator

PREFACE

Growing up as a boy in Africa I worked under the assumption that Europe was basically a Christian continent. Now that I live in Europe and have travelled extensively throughout it, I have come to realise that my initial assumption was wrong; indeed many parts of Africa could make a stronger claim to being Christian than Europe.

Christians in Europe need to wake up to this harsh reality. We are a post-Christian continent and the Church has much to do to make itself appealing and relevant once more. The job of evangelising Europe is complicated by the fact that it contains such a diverse mixture of peoples with widely differing worldviews and assumptions. All of this, I believe, has necessitated the writing of this book. It is an attempt, however inadequate, to express something of the spiritual need and diversity of this great continent.

No book is the product of just one person and so there are a number of people I would like to thank for their help in making it a reality. Even before this project began I was encouraged by the input of Peter Maiden of OM who helped me to realise the book's potential. I should also express thanks to Patrick Johnstone (who I have never met) for his work on Operation World which has been, for me, the most influential mission book I have ever read.

Within the work of GLO there are many who deserve thanks. John Speirs has been an encouragement throughout the project and Agnes Hislop was judicious in her attention to detail as she proof-read the manuscript. Three of my European colleagues were a great asset as they read the manuscript and made helpful comments. They are Pierre Bariteau (France), Juan Luis Morales (Spain) and Patrizio Zucchetto (Italy). Without their advice this book would not have been possible. Finally thanks must go to my colleagues at Tilsley College, Carolyn Baker, David

Clarkson, Mark Davies and Allison Hill who all read the manuscript and contributed to its improvement. Needless to say any mistakes are my responsibility alone. A special thanks is also owed to Mark Shufflebottom who has always been willing to do design work of the highest quality for me.

I hope this book will stimulate you to pray for Europe and to live a missional life, helping Europeans to come to a personal knowledge of Christ.

Stephen McQuoid

CONTENTS

Chapter 1
The Shape of the Past

World history is a fascinating subject, many stories can be told and key events unpacked. It is in our history that we understand where we have come from and comprehend the influences that have shaped our lives and made us what we are today. Few parts of the globe are more fascinating, however, than Europe. This ancient continent has been at the centre of world history for centuries and is as varied a place as its history is complex.

Europe is a continent that has changed and changed again. Indeed the Europe of today is almost unrecognizable from the Europe of the past, though traces of our past still remain to play their part in our generation. Europe has witnessed the rise and fall of empires. It changed its religious affiliation from paganism and superstition to Christianity; kingdoms have gradually been transformed into liberal democracies; and the political life of Europe has been filled with intrigue, rivalry, violence and revolution. It has been punctuated with wars, some of which were waged to repel invaders from outside Europe's borders, but many were between nations that comprised this continent. Some drew other nations into the conflict, while others were fought between the small tribes that vied for supremacy within national borders. All of these events have conspired to produce that eclectic patchwork that is modern Europe.

Among the many significant changes that have taken place in Europe is a change in the worldview and belief systems of Europeans. Ancient Europe was a brutish and pagan place, a continent that worshipped the Nordic gods of Thor and Oden; as well as the gods of the Greek and Roman Empires. This situation was changed forever with the advent of Christianity. The growth of Christianity within Europe is itself a complex and confusing story.

Early Christianity in Europe

The record of the beginnings of the Early Church are to be found in the book of Acts. Though these times were exciting and dramatic, the Church had its fair share of problems. There was opposition from fellow Jews and the Roman authorities, as well as other religious groups in the ancient world. Nevertheless the growth continued and the Gospel spread into Europe with Paul himself ministering in Rome, the very heart of the empire.

The early centuries were dogged with theological controversies. As the basic doctrines of the Christian faith were being explored, heresies were emerging. This was hardly surprising, after all, with the departure of the Apostles the church lacked any unifying structure and the widespread circulation of the completed canon was still some time off. The great councils of the Church played a key role in developing a coherent theology.

While all these events were taking place, persecution continued to be a reality. It would be unfair to suggest that persecution was a constant in the life of the Church, though often it was severe and politically motivated. Decius (249-251), for example, felt under pressure from the Barbarian invaders and decided that Rome must return to its ancient ways. That meant rooting out new ideas such as Christianity. Likewise Valerian (254-260) launched a fearsome and systematic persecution of the Church.

The Birth of Christendom

Change was to come, however, in the form of Constantine. In 306 Constantine succeeded his father Constantius and then proceeded to defend his throne against potential rivals. On the eve of the battle of Milvian Bridge, October 27, 312, he claimed he saw a flaming cross in the sky with an inscription in Greek reading, 'By this sign conquer'. Whether this was genuine or not, it profoundly affected Constantine and following his victory he became sympathetic towards Christianity. In March of 313 he issued an edict of toleration from Milan, restoring to the Church any confiscated property and making restitution for any other losses. This new climate that Christianity found itself in was a mixed blessing. Certainly the Church was free from persecution and free to evangelise, but the spiritual superficiality which resulted was undoubtedly destructive and led to reactionary movements such as monasticism.

Constantine's support of Christianity also meant that Europe was to become the epicentre of Christian activity.

As a more hierarchical structure was added to Church life, it became less like the simple pattern of churchmanship that we see in the New Testament. The first truly great churchman to appear in Rome since the Apostolic times was Leo the Great (390-461). The Council of Chalcedon (451) agreed to confer on him, and on his successors, the term 'Pope'. From this point onwards Leo devoted his energies to gaining universal recognition for the position of Bishop of Rome. However while this was accepted in Western Europe, Christian leaders in the East were unhappy, and this eventually led to a schism and the formation of the Orthodox Church. Though the Roman Empire crumbled and Barbarian hordes caused havoc throughout Europe, the Church would stand and its developing structure would carry through into the Middle Ages.

The Middle Ages

By the Middle Ages Christianity was well established in Europe. The ancient gods of European paganism were replaced by the God of the Bible. Europe itself had risen from the ashes of the Roman Empire and was now a continent of nations each with a strong sense of their own identity. The unity which existed within Europe was provided by the Roman Catholic Church and the strength of the Papacy. This was a time in European history when almost everyone believed in the existence of God and went to Church. The Church dominated life and involved itself in civic affairs. Great cathedrals and monasteries were being built throughout Europe and the Pope was more than just a religious leader, he was arguably the continent's most powerful political leader. His word was obeyed by princes and rulers and to disagree with him was to 'oppose God'.

There were, of course, other religious beliefs in Europe. Both Jews and Muslims lived within her borders, but they were minority faiths and often found themselves being persecuted by their Christian neighbours. No one could threaten the dominance of Christian beliefs and there was no credible alternative.

Christianity not only expressed itself through societal structures such as the monarchy and the legal system, but also through education. Whereas Europe's greatest minds had previously devoted themselves to philosophy, they were now devoting themselves to the systematising of Christianity. It was believed that everything that is known was ultimately revealed by God. This was true not just of religious knowledge, but all knowledge. In the words of Jonathan Hill, 'Faith and religion, reason and science and philosophy, were all united into a seamless body of learning'[1]. Because this learning came from God and God was believed to know everything, human knowledge was seen as a sub-set of God's divine knowledge. In His grace He chooses to disclose some of what He knows to his creatures. Because God is never wrong, this knowledge or truth that God has revealed to humans must therefore be absolute. After all, who could question the Almighty?

David Wells comments on the medieval thinkers by stating, 'They were convinced that God's revelation, of which they were custodians, was true. True in an absolute sense. It was not merely true to them; it was not merely true in their time; it was not true approximately. What God had given was true universally, absolutely, enduringly'[2]. It was this attitude to truth that made the Church the interpreter of truth and, therefore, more often that not, the builder of the universities. In effect, the Church had a stranglehold on the intellectual life of Europe.

Medieval Europe
Dominated by the Church with Christianity ruling supreme.

The Enlightenment

This situation, however, was not to last. A huge cultural change known as the Renaissance was about to sweep throughout Europe and change people's thinking forever. The Renaissance was a time of reawakening for Europe. Explorers such as Marco Polo were discovering new worlds. Polo went to the Mongol Empire and spent five years serving as a diplomat in the court of the legendary emperor Kubla Khan. He then went on to China and India before returning to Venice. His book about his exploits became arguably the most influential travel book of all time.

While these new worlds were being discovered, old ones were being brought back to life. Artists such as Michelangelo were reawakening the classical art of sculpture and painting. Increasingly non-Christian themes were being depicted as classical myths were celebrated. New techniques were being utilised like the Flemish discovery of oil paints and the Italian discovery of the rules of perspective.

Much the same was happening in the field of writing. New thinkers began to suggest that learning was an end in itself and not just something that should be done by and for the Church. Scholars began to study ancient authors, both Christian and non-Christian, and this was reflected in their writings. Erasmus, arguably the greatest scholar of his age, devoted himself to the study of ancient Greek, something which had virtually been lost in Europe. He was essentially a secular scholar who saw value in all ancient writings, not just those that were demonstrably Christian.

Perhaps the biggest change brought in by the Renaissance was the development of science. One of the key players in this regard was Francis Bacon (1561-1626). He has often been described as the first modern scientist[3]. Bacon was an extraordinary individual who was born into nobility, served as a member of parliament for Melcombe Regis, became Lord Chancellor, and then lost his seat and his freedom when accused of bribery. But it was for his contribution to science that Francis Bacon will be remembered.

Bacon sought to use experimentation as a method of opening up new discoveries. He believed that if science could be developed it would ultimately lead to a better and more contented society. His view of science was a truly noble one, for he felt that it should be used to increase the dignity and greatness of humanity. In that sense science was not just a tool of education, rather it was the gateway into Utopia.

The significance of the Renaissance lay not just in its own achievements, but also in the fact that it wedged open the door which was to lead to a period of history known as the Enlightenment. Arguably the key thinker of this period was a mathematician called René Descartes (1596-1650). Just as Bacon was viewed as the founder of modern science, Descartes was regarded as the founder of modern philosophy[4]. Born in La Haye, in France, Descartes studied law at La Fleche and Poitiers before going on to travel extensively throughout Europe, adding soldiering to his list of activities.

At Ulm, Descartes began to put his philosophical ideas down on paper, completing his first major work in the 1620's. He was a committed theist and was concerned that some thinkers during the Enlightenment were rejecting the medieval worldview of knowledge through revelation to such an extent that they were becoming sceptical about God Himself. In their quest for learning they were in effect throwing out the baby with the bathwater and rejecting Christianity as a whole and not just the medieval ideas which they had inherited. He, therefore, set out to devise a method of discovering truth that could be relied upon. The ultimate aim of this process was that he wanted to convince others of the existence of God through reason. Things, however, did not turn out the way Descartes intended.

Descartes' formulae could be summed up in the Latin phrase *Cogito ergo sum*, which means, 'I think, therefore I am'. He began by becoming more sceptical than the sceptics, by doubting everything, even to the point of doubting his own existence! Next he thought about the rationality of his position. He concluded that as he was thinking he must, therefore, actually exist irrespective of what his thoughts consisted of. The very fact that he was thinking was irrefutable proof of his existence because something that did not exist would logically be incapable of thought. He would then state that his existence was an element of objective truth that he had discovered, not because it had been revealed to him by God, but because he had discovered it simply through human reasoning. This, he considered, proved that truth could be discovered quite apart from revelation and that human rationality was a sure path towards truth. From this point Descartes would then go on to discover other truths, again without any reference to God and revelation.

The impact which Descartes had on subsequent thinking is hard to overstate. In his aftermath, divine revelation began to be replaced by human reason as the source of knowledge and truth. The result was that if someone wanted to discover the truth about a particular subject, he did so without any reference to the Church or to God. Instead he used his powers of human reason believing that this was a reliable way to new discoveries.

This new thinking began to impact all branches of knowledge, but perhaps not surprisingly, it had the biggest impact on the world of science. One proponent of this new method was Sir Isaac Newton (1642-1727). Newton believed that the universe was an orderly machine that was predictable in its function. Its operations could be understood simply by discovering the observable laws which governed it. Like Descartes, Newton was a theist and he believed that his study of the universe would lead him to wonder at the greatness of God. That, however, was not to be the experience of other scientists. They merely saw this new thinking as a pathway to truth independent of God, and in so doing they effectively deified human reason.

It would be wrong to say that medieval thinking disappeared altogether during the Enlightenment, or that the Church ceased to play an important and influential role in European life. Indeed, despite the huge cultural change that was taking place, many were still committed to the authority of the Church and believed Christianity to be true in an absolute sense. However, those who held to this viewpoint were becoming a minority. The mainstream of intellectual life followed the route that Descartes had drawn for them. The absolute grip which the Church had on the minds of Europeans was broken to such an extent that it would never again be repaired.

As we reflect on the Enlightenment it would be difficult to deny the good that this new way of thinking eventually brought, not just to Europe, but to the whole of Western society. The belief that people can make new discoveries autonomously, simply by applying their powers of reasoning, enabled the boundaries of science and engineering to be expanded. As time went by the modern world was born replete with its skyscrapers, mass transportation and a sophisticated way of life. For many this was the dawn of a new age. Mankind had progressed and was now mastering the world that he saw around him. Europeans felt particularly conscious of these developments because Europe, which was at the heart of western culture, was the dominant continent and her citizens seemed to be the pinnacle of human civilization.

Medieval Europe	Enlightenment Europe
Dominated by the Church with Christianity ruling supreme.	Truth can be discovered by reason and logic, so we don't need God.

The dissolution of autonomous man

Nothing in history is static. Cultures continually change as the events they experience impact them. The positive world of the European Enlightenment was about to be transformed by a whole series of events which would alter European thinking once more. The first of these events occurred in 1844 with the birth of a German philosopher called Friedrich Nietzsche. Born into a pious Protestant family, Nietzsche became one of Europe's most creative thinkers[5]. He studied in Bonn and Leipzig before being appointed to a professorship in Basle. As he developed his philosophy, Nietzsche declared that God was dead which meant that human beings must learn to live life without him[6].

Nietzsche began to spell out the different aspects of human existence for which man would need to assume responsibility. To begin with there was the whole issue of truth. If there was no God then there could be no objective way of testing truth. This had not been a problem for medieval thinkers because their truth claims were tested against God's Word. Neither was it a problem for people during the Enlightenment because human reason was the sure path towards truth. But for Nietzsche, rejecting both worldviews as he did, the absence of objective truth was clearly a problem. He dealt with this issue by negating the reality of truth as an absolute. In essence his feeling was that truth was what the individual made it.

However uncertain this may have seemed, Nietzsche did not seem concerned. Indeed he stated that it did not matter if a belief was true or otherwise, as long as it was 'life affirming'. In other words, if you believe something, it really does not matter whether or not what you believe is true as long as believing it does you some good and you enjoy what you believe.

A second area where, according to Nietzsche, man had to take responsibility for himself was in the area of ethics. He stated that with God out of the picture there was no basis for any objective values, meaning or significance in life.

Consequently there was no objective basis for declaring that any action was morally right or wrong. Again this would not have been the case for medieval or enlightenment thinkers. For people in the medieval world God provided an objective ethic and for enlightenment thinkers our ethical basis is developed through human reason. In both cases human ethics were objective and firm. For Nietzsche, however, this was not the case. It would be wrong to conclude that Nietzsche rejected the idea of morality altogether. Indeed he felt that morals were important, but there is no way of having an objective moral system because there was no God who could confirm the rightness of the moral system or uphold it[7]. For Nietzsche this was a logical position and he was deeply critical of philosophers who denied God's existence yet held on to their Judeo-Christian ethics.

The net result of Nietzsche's work was that a whole generation of thinkers emerged who thought human life was of little intrinsic value and that objective truth could not be found. Thus a worldview change was about to sweep through Europe once more and change the way Europeans dealt with issues of faith and belief.

The challenge of human progress

This change of worldview required more than just the writings of one philosopher. Other events conspired to make it a reality. Arguably chief among these other events were the two devastating wars, World War I and World War II, which were waged in the very heart of Europe but also involved many countries throughout the globe. It is important to understand the context in which these two great wars occurred. With the development of science there came an increased sense of expectation. It was widely believed that mankind was on an upward path towards inevitable progress. Science was beginning to answer many of life's questions and it was felt that one day it would provide answers for all of them. Man was destined to arrive at Utopia. Nowhere was this expectation more keenly felt than in Europe where science and technology had made an enormous impact. It was in this positive atmosphere that World War I exploded.

The First World War came as a huge blow to the belief in human progress. Although science had undoubtedly made a significant and positive difference to the lives of many Europeans, yet it had also produced the mustard gas which was now killing so many young men in the trenches. Once the war came to an end the path towards progress began once more, but it was short-lived. World War II brought even more carnage and once again the same science that produced so much good, also produced the V2 rocket which was tearing the heart out of civilian areas in cities such as London. Perhaps most devastating of all was the nuclear bomb which destroyed Hiroshima. As the mushroom cloud reached for the skies, people were both amazed at the technology which produced this weapon, and horrified by what this said about humanity. The dream of Utopia based on the certainties of human reason was rapidly coming to an end.

Several more things were to happen before the Enlightenment dream faded altogether. The arrival of big industry and the multinational conglomerates produced many much needed jobs in the aftermath of the great wars. But they also turned each worker into a statistic on a payroll rather than an individual. People began to lose their sense of worth as they became no more than manufacturing units on the conveyor belt of economic growth. Moreover, though big industry was the engine of the new world economy, it also caused widespread pollution and punched a hole in the ozone layer. This was progress of a sort, but it was not clean uncomplicated progress.

At the same time enlightenment thinking that produced the modern world was beginning to make an impact on architecture. Buildings began to be designed along rational lines to maximize space in an efficient way. Quaint cottages on cobbled streets were replaced by huge tower blocks made of concrete and steel. Superficially this gave the appearance of progress as affordable housing was provided for the growing populations in major cities. But these new housing developments were soulless and soon became crime-ridden. Europe was at the cutting edge of world civilisation, but at its core there was a deep sickness that was breeding discontent.

Another interesting spin-off from technological development was the formation of the global village. The world was becoming a smaller place as mass transportation became affordable. Europeans began to travel the world to see different cultures, which were found to be apparently working well. Celebrities such as the Beatles met their personal gurus, not in any of Europe's sophisticated states, but in India. Alongside the growing fascination about other parts of the world, there grew within Europe a sense that all was not well. Certainly Europe had progressed and continued to do so, but old beliefs which revelled in human rationality were steadily eroding.

The new cultural outlook which emerged has often been

labelled as post-modernism. This is now an overworked term and so I am cautious about its use, indeed I prefer to use the term 'late modernism'. However there is a need to recognise that there is a new generation of Europeans who have effectively rejected not only medieval thinking, but also enlightenment thinking in favour of their more fluid approach. These I call 'Emergent Europeans' for they represent a distinctive worldview which needs to be recognised and identified.

Medieval Europe	Enlightenment Europe	Emergent Europe
Dominated by the Church with Christianity ruling supreme.	Truth can be discovered by reason and logic, so we don't need God.	Truth does not exist in any objective way. It is the product of a person's culture and environment.

It is important to recognise that although Emergent Europeans are becoming dominant in our culture, there are nevertheless significant numbers of people within Europe who could be labelled Religious Europeans due to the influence of medieval religious thinking or Enlightenment Europeans due to the influence of Enlightenment thinking. That is, there are many Europeans who still believe in the authority of the established Church and in divine revelation, and equally, there are many Europeans who feel that human reason is supreme so there is no need to believe in God at all. These three worldviews vie for supremacy within modern Europe and provide Christians with an enormous challenge to present the Gospel in a relevant way to three entirely different kinds of people.

The new influx

The situation, however, is even more complex than this. Over the last few decades the population of Europe has been added to by significant numbers of immigrants. These I refer to as 'New Europeans'. Some of these immigrants are Christians and have brought a spiritual vitality into Europe. However, the majority of immigrants are followers of other world religions such as Islam and Hinduism. This fact adds to the challenge and makes the evangelisation of Europe an even more uphill task.

Medieval Europe	Enlightenment Europe	Emergent Europe	New Europe
Dominated by the Church with Christianity ruling supreme.	Truth can be discovered by reason and logic, so we don't need God.	Truth does not exist in any objective way. It is the product of a person's culture and environment.	Truth rests in non-Christian religions.

These then are the four Europes that we want to deal with in this book. As we do so there are two dangers that we need to be aware of. Firstly there is the danger of categorisation. While it is true that the four groups mentioned are easily identifiable in modern Europe, yet not every European will fit neatly into one of these categories. People by their very nature are complex and not always easy to define. Moreover, many Europeans will be influenced by several of the worldviews mentioned and could therefore fit comfortably into more than one of these categories.

Secondly we need to be aware of the danger of generalisation. While the traits that have been outlined are true, they are true in a general sense rather than specifically and exactly true in every situation. Within each of these world views there exists a broad spectrum and therefore precision is not possible when using such broad categories. Despite these dangers, however, this 'Four Europes" model is a useful way of identifying the kind of people who live within Europe and the challenge we face as we try to reach this continent with the Gospel.

Chapter 2
The Shape of the Present I

It is not easy to define Europe today because people mean different things when they use the name. When some people talk about Europe they are referring to the European Union (EU), a political and economic union of 25 member states which has grown since its inception and continues to do so. Others, however, use Europe in a much wider sense to include non-EU countries such as Switzerland, Iceland, San Marino and Norway. Still others, in their definition of Europe, include countries which were formerly part of the USSR, such as Russia and the Ukraine. For the purposes of this book I will be using the term Europe to include the EU member states, those countries applying for membership, some of those nations that do not wish membership and a limited number of countries in Eastern Europe. This definition, therefore, will be limited to 38 nations and will exclude Russia and the Ukraine as well as the Russian Republics.

European Union

It would be impossible, however, to deal with the issue of Europe without first mentioning the European Union. This is the biggest and most powerful political and economic alliance in Europe and one that is continuing to grow. The EU began in the 1950's as the 'European Communities', its aim to become a family of democratic European countries. The roots of the EU lay in the Second World War with a determination to prevent such killings and destruction from ever happening again. Despite the many different languages and cultures in Europe it was hoped that the EU would foster co-operation between the member states so that the values of freedom, democracy and social justice could be shared and promoted. It is now possible to cross most of the EU borders without needing a passport and without being stopped for checks. EU citizens can also live, work, study and retire in another EU country if they wish.

When the EU was inaugurated there were six member states: Belgium, Germany, France, Italy, Luxemburg and the Netherlands. This grew to nine in 1973 when Denmark, Ireland and the United Kingdom joined the founding group. Further expansion took place in 1981 and 1986 with Greece, Spain and Portugal becoming part of the burgeoning union, and in 1995 and 2004 the union was brought up to its present strength of 25. This rate of growth is likely to continue as negotiations are taking place in order to include at least four more nations.

Date	Countries
1958	Belgium, Germany, France, Italy, Luxemburg, Netherlands
1973	Denmark, Ireland, United Kingdom
1981	Greece
1986	Spain, Portugal
1990	East Germany joins in German reunification
1995	Austria, Finland, Sweden
2004	Czech Republic, Estonia, Cyprus, Latvia, Lithuania, Hungary, Malta, Poland, Slovenia, Slovakia
2007	Bulgaria, Romania
Future Plans	Croatia, Turkey

There is a rationale by which nations join the EU. Each country must be European, democratic, and committed to the concept of the union. The extent to which each country demonstrates this commitment varies. In the United Kingdom, for example, there is great suspicion about the EU and many political leaders believe they can win votes by appearing to get tough with their European counterparts. But in other European countries such as the Republic of Ireland there is a much more positive attitude towards the union.

What cannot be doubted is that the EU has become a significant entity. To begin with it has a population of 457 million – the world's third largest after China and India. As well as having a large population the EU is also the world's largest trading block. Though the EU represents only 7% of the world's population it accounts for a fifth of global imports and exports. This has resulted in a significant rise in the standard of living in EU countries. Its 100 billion annual budget has been used to create jobs and provide training for unemployed or under-qualified people. Consequently member states such as Ireland and Spain have been economically transformed in the last 20 years. However, this transition is not equal in all member states. Denmark, for example, has three times the economic output per person than that of Latvia. Nevertheless the economic success of the EU can be demonstrated in the huge numbers of asylum seekers who try to find refuge within it.

The EU has become a very advanced place to live. Education receives significant funding and more children are staying longer in education than ever before. In Finland, for example, 89.3% of 18 year olds are still in education. Educational opportunities are extended to both sexes, indeed in 2001 more women than men graduated from higher education in some disciplines. The overall standard of education has brought with it a relatively high rate of employment due to the fact that unemployment rates decrease as education attainment increases. This, however, should not mask the fact that the overall unemployment rate in the EU is 9% compared to 5.4% in the United States.

EU Higher Education Graduations 2001

Subject	Men	Women
Humanities and arts	101 016	222 340
Law	67 396	95 732
Science	172 575	124 222
Engineering, manufacturing and construction	300 233	83 675

EU member states also make use of information technology. In Denmark, for example, 69% of households and 97% of businesses have access to the internet. Many of the jobs available in the EU are linked with service industries. Agriculture by comparison employs relatively few with only 5.2% of the labour force.

The voice of the EU is its parliament. Here the 732 members of parliament sit, not in national blocks, but in seven Europe-wide political groups. The largest of these is the centre-right European People's Party (Christian Democrats), followed by the Socialists, Liberals and the Greens. Between them are all shades of opinion on European integration ranging from those who wish for a European super-state to those who are openly Eurosceptic. The main meetings of the Parliament are held in Strasbourg and Brussels and they operate in all 20 official EU languages. The main job of the Parliament is to pass European laws. The proposals for these new laws come from the European Commission which is independent of national governments and consists of 25 members (one from each EU country), supported by around 24,000 civil servants. The libertarian nature of the European Commission was emphasised recently in the debacle over the appointment of an Italian European commissioner called Rocco Buttiglione.

A bad day in Europe

The 25 members of the European Union had gathered in Rome to sign the European Constitution. It was an historic occasion, in which the famed filmmaker Franco Zeffirelli was directing live television coverage in the eternal city at the behest of Prime Minister Berlusconi, who wanted the event to be a showpiece for European democracy[8].

Italy's nomination for the European Commission was

a conservative Catholic called Rocco Buttiglione. The commission president Durao Barroso had wanted Mr. Buttiglione to serve in the Justice, Freedom and Security Post. In the course of discussions news leaked out that Mr. Buttiglione believed homosexuality to be a sin and that he had very traditional views on family values. He believed for example that marriage afforded women 'the right to have children and the protection of a man'. These views were hardly surprising for a man of deep religious conviction who came from a country that was at least nominally Catholic. They were, however, views which enraged the apparently tolerant members of the European Parliament, who threatened to vote out the entire European Commission if Mr. Buttiglione were given the position.

In a desperate attempt to save the day, Mr. Barroso telephoned both Prime Minister Berlusconi and Mr. Buttiglione and asked them to withdraw the Italian's candidacy[9]. Both men refused, insisting that Mr. Buttiglione's only crime was to have religious and moral convictions. The pressure continued to mount, however, and eventually Mr. Buttiglione seceded and withdrew. Chris Davis, leader of the British Liberal Democrat MEPs gloried in this victory. He stated, 'The European Parliament has long been criticised for lacking teeth. Today democracy has bitten back'[10]. Such, it seems, is the moral tone of the Parliament.

Arguably the most obvious sign of the European Union's strength is its development of a single currency – the Euro. Some EU countries, such as the United Kingdom, have yet to adopt the single currency, but most have, and it has meant the end of currencies such as the Franc, the Lira and the Deutschmark. The European Central Bank based in Frankfurt is responsible for managing the Euro.

THE ISLAND NATIONS
UK & IRELAND

The Island Nations

Having dealt with the monolith that is the European Union, we now want to look at some of the sub-divisions that exist within Europe. Included in this list will be non-EU countries. Though this sub-grouping is somewhat artificial it nevertheless enables us to understand the structure of Europe with more clarity.

To the north west are the isolated islands of the **United Kingdom** (UK) and Ireland. The United Kingdom consists of Great Britain (England, Scotland and Wales) and Northern Ireland. These are individual countries in their own right and each treasures its separate identity. While the whole of the United Kingdom is governed from the Parliament in London, there is currently a measure of devolution in both Scotland and Wales.

The UK was formed in 1801 as a Union of Great Britain and Ireland, with the Republic of Ireland seceding in 1921. Even before this Union, the countries of the UK were significant players on the world scene. The British Empire once covered one quarter of the world and the British Commonwealth, which still exists to this day consists of 60 independent nations. The UK was the first industrialised economy and, though less powerful now, still ranks as the world's fourth largest economy. It has also been a centre for democracy, spearheading a parliamentary system and a constitutional monarchy.

The United Kingdom has been primarily Protestant since the reign of Henry VIII. The Church of England (Anglican) is recognised as the established Church within England with the Church of Scotland (Presbyterian) playing the same role in Scotland. Blessed with revivals and outstanding Christian leaders, the UK has been a key centre of Bible-believing Christianity and for the past two centuries has been a great force for mission to the rest of Europe. However the Church is in decline and although there remains some vigorous growth within the evangelical wing of the Church, the overall picture remains somewhat gloomy. The Judeo-Christian worldview, which was held almost universally by people in the UK, is now almost totally eroded so that public opinion can no longer be described as Christian in any meaningful sense of the word.

Overall, evangelicals are holding their own, but only just. They are becoming more prominent within mainline denominations but most of the evangelical growth is happening within new Church movements. Perhaps the most exciting development has been the growth in black majority Churches. This is helped by the large numbers of Christians among the Afro-Caribbean immigrant population. However much we rejoice at this, there is also some cause for concern as many of these black majority Churches are relevant to their own communities, but are not reaching out to society at large. A recent BBC report suggested that as many as 25% of black communities are churchgoers. This is much higher than the national average and demonstrates the problem in that the particular brand of conservative Pentecostalism, which characterises many of these Churches, often makes them culturally distant from other evangelicals and the community at large.

Without doubt the future of the Anglican Church will have national repercussions. The Church of England is a kind of parent Church to the 80 million Anglicans worldwide. This Church umbrella encompasses evangelicals, liberals and Anglo-Catholics. The result of this union is that there are many divisions over issues such as homosexuality, the ordination of women and the attitude towards the Roman Catholic Church. Evangelicals are a growing force within this communion with 27% of bishops,

53% of clergy, 60% of ordinands and 40% of churchgoers claiming to be evangelical[11]. Charismatics within the Church have also contributed to a renewal process which may well, in time, change the very nature of the Church of England. At the Lambeth Conference of 1998 (the highest governing body of the Anglican Church), the liberals were defeated by the evangelicals who were buoyed on by their non-Western majority who demanded a return to Biblical values.

Although people within the UK are among the most religiously cynical in Europe, there are at least some signs of hope. Many evangelicals have been able to adapt to their rapidly changing culture and there is now a great deal of creativity evidenced in evangelism as well as a flexibility in Church life. Initiatives like the Alpha course have been a significant blessing with literally thousands of Churches using it. This good news is counterbalanced by the many evangelical Churches which are in decline, but at least it suggests that some Christians are rising to the challenge of the 21st century.

Ireland has had a very different history, both politically and spiritually. For centuries there was conflict between Protestant Britain and Catholic Ireland. This conflict has accentuated the Irish self-identity. In the 12th century Anglo-Norman nobles invaded Ireland and were eventually assimilated into Irish society. In the early 17th century, large numbers of English and Scottish Protestants began to settle into the north of Ireland. This resulted in an increase in the conflict, with Catholics rising up against their Protestant neighbours. These uprisings were brutally crushed by Oliver Cromwell.

When the monarchy was restored in 1660 and the Roman

Catholic monarch James II came to the throne, Irish Catholics hoped for better times. However, James II was deposed by the Protestant William of Orange. He then went to Ireland and tried to raise an army against the Protestant rulers. There he was defeated by William of Orange who is hailed as a saviour to this day by Protestants in Northern Ireland. Eventually after suffering widespread discrimination and famine, southern Ireland was partitioned in 1921 by an Act of Parliament and the predominantly Catholic Republic of Ireland was born.

Today Irish people are keenly aware of their history and it has given them a strongly Catholic identity. However there is no official link between the Roman Catholic Church and the State and, in general, the church's influence though strong, is on the wane. Ireland has also become very wealthy not least because of its privileged position within the EU. Arguably, however, the main reason why Irish people today do not convert to evangelical Christianity in large numbers, is not because of their strong allegiance to the Catholic Church, but rather it is due to their materialistic lifestyles.

Nevertheless, despite this apathy there are still signs of life. The Charismatic movement has had a significant impact on the nation. Though most of these charismatic Christians are within the Roman Catholic Church, they nevertheless show signs of an increased interest in the Bible and in personal spirituality. Within the Protestant tradition there has been slow but steady growth of evangelicalism. This can particularly be seen in the mainline Pentecostal denominations and the many small independent fellowships across the country. The need still remains great, however, as Ireland has the smallest proportion of evangelicals in the English-speaking world.

COUNTRY	POPULATION	LANGUAGE	NATIONAL CHURCH	EVANGELICALS
United Kingdom	59 million	English	Church of England Church of Scotland	8.5%
Ireland	3.8 million	English	Catholic	0.9%

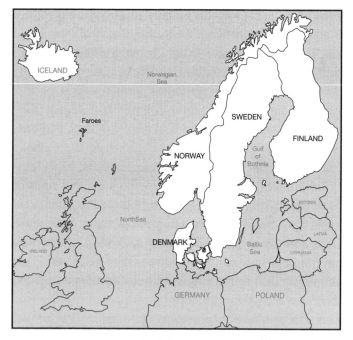

THE SCANDINAVIAN NORTH
NORWAY, ICELAND, DENMARK, SWEDEN, FINLAND, GREENLAND, FAROES

The Scandinavian North

From the Islands we move north east to the Scandinavian countries of Iceland, Norway, Sweden, Denmark and Finland. **Norway** and **Iceland** are not members of the EU but share similarities and a group identity with the other three. These nations have a Viking ancestry with Norway, **Denmark** and **Sweden** traditionally being the more powerful. Indeed **Finland** was part of Sweden up until the 19th century, while Iceland only became independent from Denmark in 1944. Scandinavia's history has not been a static one. During the time of King Canute, (11th century), for example, Norway, Sweden and England were under Danish rule. In the 13th century parts of Scotland were under Norwegian rule while Finland fell to the Russians in 1809 and remained a conquered nation until the collapse of the Russian Empire. During the Second World War Sweden remained neutral while Denmark and Norway fought the Germans in a well co-ordinated resistance movement.

Superficially the Scandinavian countries are among the most Christian in Europe. The State Church, which is Lutheran, enjoys a high membership and these countries have sent many missionaries throughout the world. However, these facts cannot mask the serious spiritual problems that exist. A combination of liberalism in the church, secularism in society and apathy mean that Scandinavia is a spiritually needy place. In Denmark, for example, while 90% of the population are members of the Lutheran Church and 50% say that they pray regularly, within most parishes attendance varies between 1% and 4%. Likewise in Sweden, though 78% of the population have been baptised as infants, less that half the population claim they still believe there is a God and only 5% go to church. In the 19th century Sweden enjoyed revivals, a vigorous Free Church movement and a huge interest in mission, but over the past century secularism has led to one of the most permissive cultures in the world. There is some evangelical growth, most notably in the newer Charismatic and Pentecostal churches, but the need is greater than ever.

Norway is a much more encouraging country from a Christian perspective. Historically it has been one of the world's great missionary sending nations and the influence of pietism has been felt for the past two centuries. The State Church (Lutheran) has many evangelical pastors, though they do struggle with their non-evangelical counterparts who, for example, campaign for homosexual freedoms within the church. The free churches, also significantly numerous, are often vibrant and are committed to church-planting.

Finland is a country of contrasts. On the one hand secular humanism has had such an influence on the national psyche that two thirds of Fins believe that life is devoid of hope. On the other hand there are many evangelicals within the state church and, while the free churches are small in number, many are vibrant and growing. Commitment is a problem though, as is the fragmentation of Christian witness.

Iceland has the smallest percentage of evangelicals in Scandinavia. The church is very nominal and affected by liberalism. New Age ideologies and the occult have had a significant impact and there are signs of a general moral decline and the disintegration of society. The main evangelical thrust comes from the Pentecostal and charismatic churches which are endeavouring to plant churches throughout the country.

Greenland as a land mass is eight times the size of the United Kingdom but its total population is less than that of an average UK town. Though linked to Denmark, Greenland has been self-governing since 1979 and its population comprises mostly of Inuit peoples. Life on this inhospitable island has always been challenging and this has been added to in recent years by very high levels of immorality, alcoholism and suicide. Almost every settlement and village has a Lutheran church, but these are mostly empty. Evangelicalism has only existed in Greenland for the past half century and there remains a great need for indigenous leadership. However, there are some encouraging signs of growth.

The tiny islands that make up the **Faroes** are the most Christian part of Scandinavia. This Danish colony with a population of under 50,000 can boast an evangelical population of 28%. There is a lack of trained leadership and structure, but churches in the Faroes still send out a significant number of missionaries. There are evangelicals within the State Church (Lutheran), though it is generally nominal. The majority of evangelicals are members of the Brethren churches which have shown consistent growth over the past century.

COUNTRY	POPULATION	LANGUAGE	NATIONAL CHURCH	EVANGELICALS
Denmark	5.3 million	Danish	Lutheran	4.8%
Faroes	42,000	Faroese	Lutheran	28.5%
Finland	5.2 million	Finnish Swedish	Lutheran	12.5%
Iceland	281,000	Icelandic	Lutheran	3.3%
Norway	4.5 million	Norwegian	Lutheran	9.3%
Sweden	8.9 million	Swedish	Lutheran	4.9%
Greenland	56500	Inuktitut	Lutheran	1.6%

THE MID WEST
GERMANY, AUSTRIA, SWITZERLAND, BELGIUM, NETHERLANDS, LUXEMBURG

The Mid West

South of Scandinavia lies the Netherlands, Germany, Austria, Switzerland and Belgium. Switzerland, is not part of the EU, but once again shares the history and culture of the nations that surround her. These countries were the heartland of the Reformation and the first European nations to send out missionaries to the non-Christian world. They were also nations which experienced a huge transformation as a result of the two world wars. The prosperity of the pre-war years were destroyed by the carnage and suffering. Consequently after the wars these nations became more concerned with building their wealth again than they were with taking Christianity to the rest of the world. Moreover the German-speaking world became a fertile ground for liberal theologians who questioned and criticised the Bible and divested it of its supernatural content.

In the aftermath of the Second World War the nations of the mid west began to recover economically. Germany, however, was divided by the Cold War, and its eastern half became known, somewhat ironically, as the German Democratic Republic. The famous Berlin Wall went up and many German families were to be divided for decades. The situation lasted until the collapse of Communism, at which point the wall was taken down and Germany was reunited.

By far the largest country in the mid west is **Germany**. It is an economic powerhouse, not just for its immediate region, but for the whole of Western Europe. Indeed Germany accounts for one third of the industrial output of the EU. Religiously Germany has been divided since the time of the Reformation. In the post-Reformation era, Catholic and Protestant princes fought against each other. Latterly, Germany was ruled both by the Catholic Hapsburgs and the Protestant Prussians. It was the Prussian Chancellor Bismarck who led Germany into the First World War.

Germany was the centre of 19th century liberal theology, and the impact of liberal theology has continued to have an effect on German churches. Many of the official Protestant Churches of Germany remain liberal. This has contributed to the overall decline of the Church which is particularly marked in what was formerly the German Democratic

Republic (East Germany) where 80% of the population are unchurched. Overall only about 3% of German men are actively involved in Church.

There are, however, large fellowship groups throughout Germany led by ministers who have neither state recognition nor theological degrees, but have effective ministries. In addition to this there are Free Churches which reflect both Charismatic and non-Charismatic spirituality. Though they represent only 1.5% of the population they are growing and a high proportion of them are evangelical. Between 1988 and 1995 some 1028 Free Churches were planted. Despite all this activity, church attendance in Germany continues to fall.

Switzerland has a unique political system and such a commitment to neutrality that it is not even a member of the United Nations. Like Germany, it is religiously divided between Catholics and Protestants, though with each region or canton enjoying a degree of autonomy the dominance of either Church group varies depending on the canton. There is, however, a decline in both traditions with church rolls being halved over the past 30 years. A lack of clergy in the Catholic Church and liberalism among Protestants have contributed to this decline. There are encouraging signs among the Evangelical and Pentecostal denominations, but they face an uphill task in this wealthy European enclave.

The **Netherlands** also has a Protestant and Catholic mix with the Protestants tending to live in the north and the Catholics in the south. Over half of the population have no link whatever with a Church and a quarter of the population classify themselves as non-religious. The nation as a whole is one of the most decadent and liberated on earth. The

Netherlands was the first country to legalise euthanasia and has become a world leader in promoting a New Age worldview. This coupled with open permissiveness and a lack of legislative restrictions makes the Netherlands a country known more for its immorality than its glorious Christian past.

Despite this, however, overall, numbers of active Christians are increasing in the Netherlands with the Charismatic renewal movement having a significant impact. There is also a strong infrastructure of Christian publishing and broadcasting, including television. In addition there has been an increased interest in mission.

Austria and Belgium are both Roman Catholic countries, but this does not tell the full story. **Austria** has seen a significant decline both in church attendance and in those wanting to be ordained into the priesthood. In the 1990's the annual membership loss from the Catholic Church was 40,000. Most people have no real connection with the church, though it is estimated that 80% of the population have had at least some dealings with the occult. The cults have also had an impact with the Jehovah's Witnesses being the third largest denomination after the Catholic and Lutheran churches. Evangelicals are a tiny minority, and since 1998, formal recognition for smaller religious groups (including Evangelicals) has been made more difficult. In 1985 there were 55 towns with populations in excess of 5000 that had no evangelical witness at all. This situation has not improved much. The Evangelical churches that do exist struggle to find pastors and the church is heavily dependant on foreign help.

Belgium likewise has seen dwindling support for the Catholic Church. While 90% of the population would be classified as Catholic, only one in ten actually attend Mass. Meanwhile the cults, the occult and neo pagans have attracted a great deal of attention. As a nation it is deeply divided between the Waloons in the south and east and the Flemish in the north and west. Catholic culture is the one common denominator but its influence is negligible and incapable of uniting the country.

The Evangelical church is experiencing growth, but it is slow and is hampered by a lack of Christian workers and pastors. For example, only 40% of Flemish speaking congregations have an indigenous pastor. Undeterred, however, some of the evangelical denominations are working towards further church-planting despite it being a slow and difficult process. In the year 2000, for example, the Flemish Pentecostals launched a vision of planting 120 churches by the year 2015.

Luxemburg is a tiny enclave whose significance lies, at least in part, in the fact that it is a base for several EU institutions. With a population of less than half a million this tiny parliamentary monarchy is the smallest member of the European Community. Though traditionally a Catholic country, most people in Luxemburg do not actively practice their faith and secularism as well as the New Age Movement plays an important role in society. The Jehovah's Witnesses have made greater inroads than any evangelical group and many of the Evangelicals who live in Luxemburg are foreigners.

COUNTRY	POPULATION	LANGUAGE	NATIONAL CHURCH	EVANGELICALS
Germany	8.2 million	German	Catholic Protestant (EKD)	2.9%
Austria	8.2 million	German	Catholic Reformed Churches	0.4%
Switzerland	7.4 million	German French Italian Rheto-Roman	Catholic Protestant	4.1%
Belgium	10.1 million	Flemish French German	Catholic	1.1%
The Netherlands	15.8 million	Dutch Frisian	Catholic Protestant	4.5%
Luxembourg	440,000	Letzebuergesch French German	Catholic	0.3%

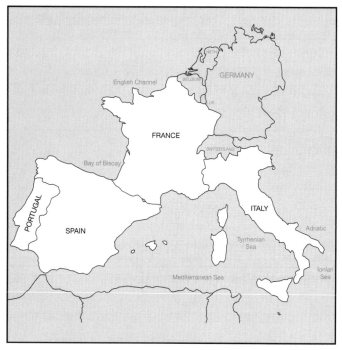

THE SUNSHINE STATES
FRANCE, SPAIN, PORTUGAL, ITALY

Chapter 3
The Shape of the Present II

The Sunshine States

Along the shores of the Mediterranean lie the sun kissed lands of Europe. These include France, Spain, Portugal and Italy. These are amongst the most spiritually needy countries within Europe.

France is the second largest country in Europe, and also one of the most influential. The French are proud of themselves, their intellectual achievements and their sophistication. The French Revolution of 1789 had a dramatic impact on the nation, and today France is a secular state which allows freedom of religion. Although three quarters of French people claim to be Roman Catholics only about 10% attend church on a regular basis and 20% are baptised as infants. The many religious conflicts that have taken place in French history have left French people generally cynical towards organised religion. There is also a significant section of the population that would consider itself non-religious (possibly 20%) and a vigorous, growing Muslim population. Perhaps surprisingly the occult is very popular in France. There are 50,000 full-time black arts practitioners, a statistic that well outnumbers full-time Christian workers.

Protestantism in France is very much weaker than it used to be. During the Reformation almost half the population were Protestant and this resulted in the formation of the Huguenots. Subsequently conflict between the Huguenots and Catholic groups led to civil war. Protestants were then persecuted by the Catholic authorities which led to 200,000 fleeing the country for sanctuary. The persecution culminated in the slaughter of 3,000 Huguenots in Paris on 22 August, 1572. The trauma of this event led to the granting of religious tolerance in 1589. Most Protestants today are found in the north east and the south east and many of these suffer from nominalism.

Huge areas of French society are almost untouched with the Gospel. Indeed many French people will never come across a Christian in their lifetime. 50 million French people have no real link with a Christian church. In France, there is only one Evangelical church for every 33,000 inhabitants and in total less than 2,000 churches. Missionary work in France is made difficult by the fact that the French see themselves as Europe's cultural leaders, and are therefore reticent to listen to foreigners. Moreover the insensitivity of the Anglophone nations, especially the UK and the USA, has meant that many French people view evangelical Christianity as a quasi-imperialistic cultural form. There is also a great deal of suspicion about 'sects' within France and this also impinges on how French people view Evangelicals.

Despite the enormous challenge which France presents to the Gospel, there are also some encouragements. Evangelical

Christianity has been growing steadily, if not spectacularly, for the past sixty years. In 1940 the total number of Protestants in France was only 40,000. However, by 1980 the Evangelical community alone numbered 27,000. By the year 2000 the number of Evangelicals had risen yet again to 488,000. This is still very small compared to the overall population, but the statistics continue to go in the right direction.

Italy was Europe's most powerful country during the time of the Roman Empire, but with the Barbarian invasions its power decreased and Roman civilisation was in ruins by the 5th century. The legacy which Italy has left the world is enormous – Roman law, the Latin language, culture and innovation. Following the collapse of the empire, Italy then became a loose connection of independent city states right up until the 19th century when it united to become a republic. During the First World War the Italians fought with the Allies against the Germans, but when Benito Mussolini's Fascist party seized power, they switched sides and ended up fighting with the Nazis during the Second World War. Mussolini was a ruthless dictator and after the allied invasion of Italy, he found himself under arrest.

Italy's recent history has been dogged by a continual struggle with the Catholic Church and the Communists. As a country Italy has never enjoyed political stability. It became a Republican democracy in 1946 but most governments have been short lived and riddled with corruption. Indeed there have been a total of 60 governments since the Second World War. One of the most constant features of Italian society is the Mafia which controls the black market and wields significant power. Successive governments and the judiciary have tried to stamp out this menace but with little success. Extortion alone feeds the Mafia to the tune of US$23 billion per year. The troubles of this nation make it hard to believe that it performed such a huge role in the development of European law, language and culture.

The Catholic Church is still dominant in the national psyche, though it is estimated that 10 million people have left the church in this generation. Moreover the Catholic Church ceased to be the state religion in 1984. The occult and the cults are growing rapidly. There are thought to be three times more magicians than Catholic priests, and the total number of Evangelicals is less than Jehovah's Witnesses. Evangelicals are more numerous in the poor south than they are in the prosperous north. On the whole they are weak and scattered, with only 500 of Italy's 33,500 communities having an established witness.

To the south of France lies the country of **Spain**. This is a land of remarkable history and diversity. For much of its history Spain has been a strongly Roman Catholic country, though for six centuries it was dominated by the Islamic Moors and Arabs. Later on in the 15th and 16th centuries Spain became powerful and wealthy and began colonising other parts of the world, particularly Latin America.

The Spanish monarchy was overthrown in 1931 when a new socialist republic tried to limit the power of the Catholic Church. This was followed by a revolt in 1936 against the socialists led by General Franco. He had the support of both Germany and Italy as they shared his fascist ideology. The bloody Civil War continued for three years (from July 1936 to April 1939) and the divisions caused by it were exacerbated by Franco's use of German bombers. During his reign the Catholic Church was the state religion and

Evangelicals found themselves being discriminated against.

Franco remained in power until his death in 1975. His support of Germany and Italy during the Second World War made him unpopular abroad, and the repressiveness of his regime made him unpopular at home. Under his reign Spain saw very little economic development or religious freedom. With Franco deposed Juan Carlos de Bourbon became king, and the country made a gradual move towards the full democracy which it now enjoys.

The vast majority of Spanish people would be Roman Catholic with 4% calling themselves non-religious. Only a third of the population, however, attends church (though this is one of the highest proportions in Europe). It would not be an understatement to suggest that the Catholic Church is in crisis. Few are applying for the priesthood pushing the average age of priests to 57. In 1960 there were 23,000 students in seminary; by 1999 the number had dropped to 2000. Perhaps the only growth area is the Charismatic movement within the Catholic Church which has some 35,000 active members meeting in 650 groups.

Spain is rapidly becoming a very secular society, not least because of its chequered religious past. This leads to some conflict between the secularisers and the traditional Catholics within Spain who tend to be conservative. Although complete religious freedom was granted in 1978, there is still a great deal of prejudice towards Protestants. Evangelicals are also sometimes mistaken for Jehovah's Witnesses who are active throughout Spain. The Jehovah's Witnesses are the largest non-Catholic grouping.

The growth of Spanish Evangelicals is encouraging, though slow. Spain has never experienced a revival and is greatly in need of one. Evangelicals also need to come out from under the shadow of their despised minority status and use their religious freedom to the full. There are also a couple of other issues that the Evangelical community need to deal with. Firstly, they need to make their churches truly indigenous as many of the missionaries to Spain have unwittingly imported their own national idiosyncrasies into the churches they have planted. Secondly, Evangelicals need to work together in a more unified way.

Portugal is Spain's immediate neighbour to the west. Though originally part of Spain, Portugal became independent in the 12th century and became one of the major colonising powers before facing decline. In 1910 Portugal became a republic but suffered a military coup in 1926. From then until 1968 it was ruled in a fairly dictatorial manner by Prime Minister Salazav. Another coup in 1974 brought about a coalition government and the restoration of democracy, and shortly after this the Portuguese colonies (Mozambique, Angola, Guinea-Bissau, São Tomé and Cape Verde) were granted their independence.

It was only after the coup of 1974 that religious freedom was granted in Portugal, though the Roman Catholic Church still retains some privileges. Some groups like the Jehovah's Witnesses and Mormons have seen dramatic growth since then, but many evangelical groups have faired less well. The Evangelical Church has suffered division and has also struggled with the dominance of Catholicism. Evangelicals are still regarded by many in Portugal as a sect. The situation has been further complicated in recent years by Portugal's economic development which owes much to its membership of the EU. This development has made the country more materialistic and less interested in spiritual matters. The Catholic Church has lost some of its grip on the country as a result of this development. This is most marked in central and southern Portugal.

As the Evangelical Church in Portugal looks to the future there are many challenges. There is a great need to heal some of the divisions that have been caused by such issues as prosperity teaching. The Evangelical Alliance with its growing presence might have a role to play here. There is also a need to rise to the challenge of mission. By virtue of the widespread use of the Portuguese language the Evangelical Church is in a strategic position. However there is relatively little response in this direction. There is also a lack of trained leadership and full-time workers. In spite of these problems there are nevertheless signs of growth among Portuguese Evangelicals, especially among the Pentecostals and Charismatics.

COUNTRY	POPULATION	LANGUAGE	NATIONAL CHURCH	EVANGELICALS
France	59.1 million	French	Catholic	0.8%
Spain	39.7 million	Castilian	Catholic	0.4%
Portugal	9.8 million	Portuguese	Catholic	3.1%
Italy	57.2 million	Italian	Catholic	0.9%

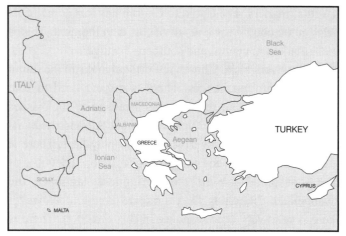

THE AEGEAN AND MID-MEDITERRANEAN

GREECE, TURKEY, CYPRUS, MALTA

Aegean and Mid-Mediterranean

Turkey is unusual amongst the nations of Europe in that it is almost entirely Islamic. Although some Turks do not consider themselves to be European, it has nevertheless applied for EU membership on several occasions, and inclusion in the near future seems likely[12]. Geographically, Turkey being linked to both Europe and Asia finds itself in a strategic location, though this adds complexities as tension exists between Turkey and almost all of its neighbours.

Though officially secular, it is overwhelmingly Muslim with the Christian population numbering only in the thousands. In the days of the Ottoman Empire, Turkey was the guardian of Islam's holy places and its chief protagonist. The Orthodox Church has a modest presence in Turkey and

Evangelical Christianity, which is growing, is still very small. As recently as 1960 there were only a dozen Evangelicals in the country. By the year 2000 there were 34 fellowships with a membership of about 2000; by 2003 there were 3,000 Evangelicals meeting in 76 fellowships and the number continues to rise at a measured pace. With some sections of the Muslim population becoming increasingly radicalised there is an ongoing hostility towards Christianity.

Officially there are no missionaries in Turkey, though many have gone as tent-makers and are beginning to make inroads. However the job is monumental and there is much to be done. One important focal point is literature. Istanbul has a much visited Christian bookshop run by the Bible Society and there are also seven Turkish Christian publishing houses which produce Bibles and a limited number of Christian book titles. Legally Turkey allows freedom of religion, but in practice this does not amount to very much, and Christians find it very difficult to witness in that environment.

On Turkey's western front lies Greece. In 1827 Greece became independent after nearly 400 years of Turkish rule. Tensions with Turkey still exist, and Greece has also been troubled with two civil wars and two dictatorships in the past fifty years. Today Greece is a republic and a parliamentary democracy. Like Turkey it is a member of NATO, but unlike its neighbour it already has EU membership which has brought stability, modernisation and commerce. Greece has the largest shipping fleet in the EU and a growing tourist industry.

Greece is predominantly Greek Orthodox. There is a measure of religious freedom though ongoing opposition and discrimination remain, and this affects the small Evangelical community which numbers only 15,000.

During the years of Turkish and then German occupation, the Orthodox Church became a focal point for Greeks. Consequently the Orthodox faith has become part of the Greek identity and all other groups are treated with suspicion. The perception is that to leave the Orthodox Church is to become less Greek, and therefore a threat to the Greek way of life. This makes evangelistic work very difficult. There are some true believers within the Orthodox Church but they are few and far between.

Among the most spiritually needy people in Greece are the immigrants and the island communities. There are approximately 150 Greek islands that have no resident Christian witness. Two possible solutions exist which will help to meet this great need. Firstly, there is literature work which has proved very successful in Greece. Secondly, there are many Greeks who live abroad (USA 2 million, Germany 500,000, Australia 272,000). Within these communities there are Evangelical churches and this could provide a source of missionaries to reach their spiritually impoverished homeland.

Cyprus became a divided nation in 1974 due to the Turkish invasion and occupation of part of the island. In the north there is the Turkish Republic of Northern Cyprus, and in the south there is the Republic of Cyprus which is Greek speaking and still lays claim to the whole island. The partition has caused deep and bitter divisions with little sign of any kind of resolution. The Republic of Cyprus has fared better economically than its northern counterpart which relies heavily on Turkish subsidies. Spiritually however it is needy.

The Orthodox Church is seen as the guarantor of Greek Cypriot culture and so the boundary between politics, culture and Church is blurred. Attendance is high at 48%

and traditionalism is strong. Evangelicals number only a few, even though Cyprus is an important base for Christian organisations. There are vibrant Churches in the ethnic minority communities such as the English-speaking peoples and the Filipinos. These need to reach out to the indigenous population. The Turkish Republic of Northern Cyprus is overwhelmingly Islamic and therefore also very spiritually needy.

Malta is the last of the sunshine states, but like the rest, it is a spiritually needy place. It was one of the first European nations to embrace Christianity after the Apostle Paul was shipwrecked on the island. Church attendance in Malta is relatively high with almost 90% of the population adhering to Catholicism, however, few have any personal faith in Christ and most of the Catholic Churches tend to be very traditional. Catholic charismatic groups have spread throughout the country and these might well provide openings for a more Bible-centred Christianity.

Until Independence in 1964 there was no Evangelical or Protestant witness as the British authorities did not allow it. Since then there has been slow but steady growth. There are now 11 congregations with 500 members. Not only does Malta need the Gospel, but it is also a strategic meeting place for the many Libyans and Tunisians travel through Malta.

COUNTRY	POPULATION	LANGUAGE	NATIONAL CHURCH	EVANGELICALS
Greece	10.6 million	Greek	Orthodox	0.4%
Turkey	70.0 million	Turkish	Islam	0.01%
Cyprus	800,000	Greek Turkish	Orthodox Islam	0.2%
Malta	390,000	Maltese English	Catholic	1.0%

CENTRAL AND EASTERN EUROPE

POLAND, HUNGARY, BULGARIA,
CZECH REPUBLIC, SLOVAKIA, ROMANIA,
CROATIA, BOSNIA, ALBANIA, SLOVENIA,
SERBIA & MONTENEGRO, MACEDONIA

Central and Eastern Europe

We now come to a part of Europe that has only recently reopened to mission activity, that is those countries that were previously behind what Winston Churchill once described as the 'iron curtain'.

We begin with **Poland** which is on Germany's eastern border. Poland became a nation in the 11th century, but its history has been one of occupation and hardship. Most recently, during World War II one quarter of the population lost their lives. This was followed by a period of communism which was in turn reversed with the Solidarity protests, resulting in the formation of a multi-party democracy in 1989.

Since the fall of communism Poland has prospered. It became a member of NATO in 1999 and then joined the EU in 2004. With its programme of economic reform, Poland has transformed itself into one of the most robust economies in central Europe. Despite this progress Poland remains very spiritually needy. There is freedom of religion but the Catholic Church is powerful and actively asserts this power in Polish society. It is also very conservative and has a strong theological commitment to the veneration of Mary and the saints. The vast majority of Poles are Catholic and see the Church as the custodian of Polish culture. However, with the ending of communism and the reforms which have benefited Poland, it seems as if Poles are less in need of Catholicism as a focal point in their lives. Consequently attendance which was at 58% in 1989 has now dropped to 23%. The church has tried to flex its political muscle to maintain a position of prominence, but this has backfired and its popularity has declined in tandem with its efforts to assert itself.

Evangelicals are only a tiny minority and they still suffer low level discrimination and are often seen as a sect. This confusion is compounded by the fact that the Jehovah's Witnesses are very active in Poland and far outnumber Evangelicals who have also often been divided. However the formation of an Evangelical Alliance in 1999 has brought hope of unity. There are also modest efforts to church plant and some strategic research is taking place to facilitate this. As young Polish people are eager to learn, teaching English is one of the great opportunities that exist as a means to bridge-building.

Lying to the south of Poland are the **Czech Republic** and **Slovakia** which formed Czechoslovakia until they separated in 1993. Four years previously they were freed from communism as a result of a bloodless revolution. Since then both countries have struggled to transform themselves into modern free market economies. There is potential for future prosperity, but more radical reforms are necessary. From a spiritual perspective the needs are just as great. Both countries allow freedom of religion, and in each case the Catholic Church predominates. However secularism is a potent force and the Church's influence is tempered by that.

Evangelicals are few in number and have much to do to win their fellow countrymen. Protestants (including Evangelicals) in the Czech Republic are experiencing life free from persecution for only the second time since 1620. Protestantism has played an important role in the country's history, but there is a need for more purity. However, there is encouraging evidence of some lives being changed as a result of charismatic renewal. There is also a considerable shortage of quality trained leadership and this, no doubt, contributes to the lack of evangelistic zeal.

Slovakia also has a strong Christian heritage but is finding that both Catholicism and Protestantism are declining. Evangelicals suffer from an inferiority complex and although some groups are growing, others are merely in survival mode. There is a great need for a renewed vision among Evangelicals. There is also a need for training though some is being provided by the Evangelical Alliance. Slovakia also has some sizable minorities, most notably Hungarians and Gypsies but these groups are proving more difficult to reach.

Further to the south are **Hungary** and Romania. Prior to 1918 the Austro-Hungarian Empire was one of the great powers in Europe. It then experienced a break up, with current day Hungary occupying only 40% of its former empire. During World War II the communists became an occupying power and remained until 1990. This period saw a great deal of tragedy not least during the 1956 uprising when 80,000 Hungarians were killed and a further 200,000 fled to the West.

Since becoming a multi-party democracy Hungary has joined NATO (1999) and the EU (2003). It has also developed economically and has enjoyed an increased standard of living. There is freedom of religion, and though the Catholic Church is the largest in the country, there is a sizable Protestant minority. Evangelicals are not numerous, and they struggle with some major issues including a lack of godly leadership. Despite this, however, there are more Evangelicals in Hungary than in many of the neighbouring countries, indeed there is not a single town in Hungry without an Evangelical congregation. Moreover there are definite signs of spiritual hunger in the country despite resistance to the gospel in much of the country.

Romania is a country that has suffered as a result of the greed of its leaders. Rich in oil and agriculture, this wealth was squandered during the communist era. Today Romania still lags behind some of its former iron curtain neighbours due to a lack of radical economic reforms. From a spiritual point of view, however, Romania fares better than most.

The largest church in the country is the Orthodox Church, but both Protestants and Catholics have a significant presence. There is more religious freedom now than there was under communism, though there is some opposition from the Orthodox Church towards religious minorities including Evangelicals. Interestingly there is a renewal movement within the Orthodox Church called the Lord's Army which numbers some 300,000 and has close links with the Romanian Evangelical Alliance.

Evangelicals in Romania have often lacked unity. However there is some growth and many new churches are being planted, though there is a great need for trained leaders. Within Romania the Gypsies are a despised minority and were spiritually isolated. However outreach to Gypsies is on the increase and this has been helped by the recent completion of the Bible in Kalderash. There are also significant spiritual needs in the south east where there are far fewer churches that in the north west.

Yugoslavia was one nation under communist rule but, after the death of Tito (1980) and the collapse of communism, it divided up into five separate republics. This was followed by the Balkan wars which devastated the region and precipitated UN involvement. This is the most ethnically diverse part of Europe and the conflict has served to entrench existing prejudices. Slovenia has developed the most economically due to its developing trading links with central and western Europe. It has a strong Catholic tradition but little spiritual vitality. Nominalism is on the increase and atheism is widespread. Evangelicals are a tiny minority and lack trained leadership. One bright ray of hope is the new translation of the Bible which the Bible Society has just completed. All Christian groups are working together to ensure its widespread distribution through schools and secular bookshops.

Bosnia was Europe's second poorest country before the Balkan war. The war shattered its agrarian economy and now foreign aid is virtually the only source of income. Culturally Bosnia straddles East and West. During the five hundred year Turkish occupation most Bosnians became Muslim. The Serb, Croat, Bosnian war caused immense damage to Bosnia and the country suffered partition. Today an uneasy peace is held together by NATO troops. Theoretically there is religious freedom, however, the scars run deep and consequently this is not so in practice. Life is a real struggle for Evangelicals though there is some growth. In 1991 there were 3 congregations and by 2000 this had grown to 29 with about 700 attending. Evangelicals have gained some credibility for their role in bridge-building between the different ethnic groups.

Croatia and **Serbia** were bitter rivals in the coalition that was Yugoslavia. During the Balkan war Croatia lost a lot of its territory to Serbia but regained it again through diplomacy. Hatred of Serbs and Bosnians is still a prominent feature of national life. With the link between ethnicity and religion in the region, Croats have become spiritually resistant in their commitment to Catholicism. However Evangelicals have been able to relate to all the ethnic groups and this has produced results. There is need for church planting, but what growth there is has been encouraging. Croatia and the whole region has been greatly helped by the Evangelical Theological Seminary in Osijek which has become a large interdenominational school producing a generation of Christian workers.

Serbia and **Montenegro** are united by Orthodox Christianity, but by little else. The Montenegrins are embarrassed by their association with Serbia and are fiercely independent, so the two nations exist in an uneasy federation. In both nations there is a fragile democracy, and the growing strength of the Serbian Orthodox Church could cause problems, not least in the realm of religious freedom.

Protestants number a little over 100,000 and Evangelicals are few in number, especially among Serbs. Most Evangelicals come from minority communities. There is a lack of unity among Evangelicals though the Evangelical Alliance has a role to play. In addition there are few trained leaders. The KES Bible School which is interdenominational but has links with the Brethren and Baptists has an important role to play. However it is small, needs funding, has a limited curriculum and relies heavily on foreign input.

People in Montenegro remain deeply divided as to whether or not it is wise to bid for complete independence from Serbia, and the situation remains volatile as a result. The orthodox faith here is nominal, while at the same time Evangelicalism is minute, limited to only 5 churches and 300 believers. The spiritual needs of this tiny mountainous enclave could hardly be overstated.

Macedonia is the final part of the jigsaw that is the Balkans, and one of the poorest. The dominant feature of the political and social fabric of this nation is its ethnic diversity. Finding a balance that keeps everyone happy is all but impossible. Of particular concern are the Albanians who are Muslim. They make up one third of the population, are growing in number due to a higher birth-rate, and are demanding more rights. The Orthodox Church, though weak, is the dominant religious grouping. The churches are largely empty and there are only 150 priests to serve the whole country. Evangelicals are a tiny minority, but they are growing. Foreign missions have also taken a real interest in Macedonia and are working alongside national believers, but this is one of the most difficult countries in Europe to access.

Albania is the last and poorest country on this list. Like Bosnia it has a large Muslim population and its proximity to the Balkans has meant that it has been adversely affected by their troubles. It remains an unstable country struggling to get to grips with democracy. In the midst of the chaos that is Albania, the Gospel has had an impact. Evangelical Christians are a small but growing minority. Under the tyrannical rule of Enver Hoxha no religion was allowed to exist and he made the proud boast that he would eliminate all religion. He failed and now 74% of the population claim to believe in God.

Evangelicals, such as there were, were persecuted severely under communism, and even though life is still not easy for them, there is a new optimism and vibrant congregations are now becoming a reality. By 1999 the handful of Evangelical Christians had grown to over 1000, meeting in a couple of dozen churches and fellowship groups. By 2000 there were 55 denominations represented in 130 congregations and 55 fellowship groups. 60% of all Evangelical churches are linked with the Albanian Evangelical Alliance. The distribution of the Bible has been vital and a new translation was completed in 1993.

COUNTRY	POPULATION	LANGUAGE	NATIONAL CHURCH	EVANGELICALS
Poland	38.8 million	Polish	Catholic	0.2%
Hungary	10.0 million	Hungarian	Catholic Protestant	2.7%
Bulgaria	8.3 million	Bulgarian Turkish	Orthodox	2.0%
Czech Republic	10.2 million	Czech	Catholic	1.1%
Slovakia	5.4 million	Slovak	Catholic	1.5%
Romania	22.3 million	Romanian	Orthodox	6.3%
Croatia	4.4 million	Croatian	Catholic Orthodox	0.5%
Bosnia	4.0 million	Bosnian	Muslim Orthodox Catholic	0.07%
Albania	3.2 million	Albanian	Muslim Orthodox Catholic	0.3%
Slovenia	1.9 million	Sloven Hungarian Italian	Catholic	0.2%
Former Yugoslavia (Serbia & Montenegro)	10.7 million	Serbian	Orthodox	1.4%
Macedonia	2.1 million	Macedonian	Orthodox	0.2%

Chapter 4
Thinking about Religious Europeans

What kind of people are we likely to encounter in this new Europe? This is a vital question to ask. If we are able to give even a tentative answer to the question then we can be prepared to make our impact on this continent, for to be forewarned is to be forearmed. So who will we meet as we go out in mission?

The first group of people we will meet is the Religious Europeans. These are the people who maintain a commitment to the established churches, namely, Roman Catholic, Lutherans, Orthodox and Anglican. Although in general these churches are in decline in Europe, they still have a significant presence. It is, therefore, important to have some kind of understanding of the beliefs and presuppositions of adherents.

Roman Catholic Church

Any study of Christian belief within Europe must begin with Roman Catholicism as this is the largest denomination within Christendom. The Roman Catholic Church has approximately one billion adherents, with significant growth taking place in Latin America and Africa. In Europe the Catholic Church has lost a lot of ground, though it would still be the most prominent religious movement in countries such as France, Spain, Portugal, Italy and the Republic of Ireland.

There is an inherent danger in trying to define what Roman Catholics believe. The Roman Catholic Church is very large and contains a huge diversity of opinion. Under the umbrella of Catholicism there are liberals, conservatives, mystics, charismatics and even some who appear to be Evangelical in outlook. This diversity was apparent in the recent appointment of Pope Benedict XVI. The conservatives in the church were delighted because he took a traditional stance on doctrinal matters. For liberals within the church, however, there was great disappointment. They wanted a Pope who would take a more conciliatory attitude towards homosexuals as well as one who would be more flexible on the issue of the ordination of women. Meanwhile the Evangelical wing within the church, while delighted with a Pope who would promote ethics, would have preferred one who was less strident in his opposition to other denominations.

Perhaps the best way forward is to identify some of the key doctrines which have 'official' recognition in the Catholic Church. I will focus my remarks on two doctrines which Evangelical Christians would disagree with and deliberately ignore the many areas where Catholics and Evangelicals are much more in agreement. This will enable us to understand something of the theology of the Roman Catholic Church while identifying where it falls short of Biblical standards. The two areas that I will focus on are those of the source of authority for the church and the doctrine of salvation.

Source of Authority

The first area that we need to identify is that of authority. The Roman Catholic Church, like its Protestant counterparts, believes in the inspiration of Scripture. To that extent there is an undoubted commitment to the Bible as the Word of God. However, whereas most Protestant denominations would see the Bible as being the only authority for faith and practice, the Roman Catholic Church relies heavily on what it calls its 'tradition'.

This body of tradition consists of the 15 apocryphal books, the writings of the Greek and Latin Fathers, a huge collection of Church Council pronouncements, and Papal Decrees. While the Roman Catholic Church sees this tradition as distinct from Scripture, nevertheless, the relationship between the two is strong. The Catechism describes it in this way, 'Both of them, flowing out of the same divine well-spring, come together in some fashion to form one thing and move towards the same goal'[13]. While there is much in this body of tradition that is helpful, it is also true to say that some of it is theologically wrong and is a contradiction of Scripture. This commitment to tradition therefore obscures Biblical truth and effectively misleads communicants.

Another related difficulty with this system is that the Church puts itself forward as the interpreter of truth. The catechism states, 'The task of giving an authentic interpretation of the Word of God, whether in its written form or in the form of Tradition, has been entrusted to the living, teaching office of the Church alone. This means that the task of interpretation has been entrusted to the bishops in communion with the successor of Peter, the Bishop of Rome'[14]. In other words, it is not up to the individual to read the Bible for himself and determine what is or is not true. The job of deciding truth and communicating it to people rests with the institution of the Church and therefore is ultimately the responsibility of the Pope and his bishops. This means that truth is a closed shop. Communicants simply have to accept what they are taught and in receiving this body of truth they are subject both to Scripture and Tradition. The difficulty is that, in practice, false doctrines have been accepted as a result of tradition being believed instead of Scripture.

Doctrine of Salvation

The second major area where this problem has occurred is in the doctrine of salvation. The Bible is unambiguous in this area, declaring that we are saved by grace through faith and that we do not contribute in any way to our salvation (Eph.2:8,9). Catholic doctrine is somewhat more convoluted.

The Roman Catholic Church does recognise the work of Christ on the cross as something which is vital to our salvation. The cross is a symbol of God's love for us, indeed, 'his plan for us is one of benevolent love, prior to any merit on our part'[15]. The cross also achieves two things. Firstly it achieves definitive redemption for men and secondly it restores man to communion with God[16]. But here the story does not end. Though we rely on Christ for our salvation, we nevertheless have to perform some works of our own to earn salvation. These works include the use of the sacraments. The sacraments act *ex opera operato* that is, they work by the very fact of the action being performed and they are necessary for salvation[17]. We will not look at all seven of the Roman Catholic sacraments but merely focus on three[18].

Firstly there is the issue of baptism which the Catholic Church claims was tied to the issue of forgiveness by Christ himself during the great commission[19]. The act of baptism cleanses the person being baptised so completely, 'that there remains in us nothing left to efface, neither original sin nor offences committed by our own will'[20]. In other words, once the child has been baptised, the effects of sin are effectively dealt with and baptism is seen as part of the salvation process. It does not deliver the person from the struggles he will have with sin for the rest of his life, these subsequent sins are dealt with in other ways, but at least baptism has provided an initial guarantee of forgiveness for the new-born child.

Baptism is then followed at a later date by confirmation. The assumption is that by this stage the person has been baptised into the Roman Catholic Church and is therefore a Christian. Needless to say this process has not required any faith on the part of the person in question, but has depended on the interest and faith of the parents to baptise him. The idea behind confirmation is that the person receives the seal of the Holy Spirit which is essential for him to live a good life. It is the equivalent in the life of an individual to the pouring out of the Holy Spirit which occurred at Pentecost[21]. The result is that the person is brought more fully into relationship with God, is gifted with spiritual gifts, and makes the relationship with Jesus

Christ a more perfect one. It also has the effect of bringing to completion whatever was started by baptism. Once again it brings spiritual advancement through a physical action.

This now brings us to the Eucharist, the celebration of the Lord's Supper. In Roman Catholic terminology it is described as the, 'source and summit of the Christian life'[22]. A great emphasis is given to the Eucharist because it is believed that communicants experience the 'real presence' of Christ as they partake of the bread. The bread and wine literally become the body and blood of Christ. In the words of the Catechism, 'In the most blessed sacrament of the Eucharist the body and blood, together with the soul and divinity, of our Lord Jesus Christ and, therefore, the whole Christ is truly, really, and substantially contained'[23]. In other words, the bread and wine are not mere symbols but the real and physical person of Christ.

This conversion of bread and wine into the body and blood of Christ is called transubstantiation and this occurs during the Eucharistic ceremony at the point of consecration. Christ is wholly present in each part of the bread (or wafer) so that he is not divided when it is broken and distributed. Once the bread is transformed into the body of Christ it continues to be that. This necessitates it being kept in a container called a tabernacle for purposes of storage. It is never thrown out. The tabernacle is therefore venerated, often kept in a special place within church buildings. Its presence within the Church building is a continual reminder to communicants of his presence within the Church.

The Eucharistic celebration has several significant theological implications. Two of these are worth noting. Firstly, it is a sacrifice. It is literally believed that when the celebration takes place Christ is crucified once more, or in the words of the catechism, 'the sacrifice of the cross is perpetuated'[24]. Secondly, in receiving the host (bread) communicants are literally receiving Christ. This action not only unites them with Christ but it also cleanses from past sin and preserves from future sin[25]. In this way it forms part of the work of redemption[26].

It is clear from this short critique that Roman Catholic theology has departed from Biblical teaching. Undoubtedly its long history, its respect for tradition and its chequered leadership has contributed to this departure. Its theological stance is also so entrenched that it is difficult to see how any kind of significant reformation can take place. It is therefore important that we endeavour to communicate the simplicity of the Gospel message to Roman Catholics. In saying this I am not suggesting that Roman Catholics cannot be true Christians. On the contrary I believe there are many committed Roman Catholics who enjoy a genuine relationship with Jesus Christ and have a real and a living faith. However the false teaching of the church certainly provides a real barrier to genuine faith and this necessitates the evangelisation of Catholics. Moreover it would also be true to say that a great many Catholics are that in name only. They attend Church irregularly and only out of habit or custom. For many there is no real attempt to engage with God, He is merely seen as the one who absolves sin rather than an intimate friend and Lord.

Engaging with Catholicism

As we engage in this evangelism there are a number of

things that we need to be aware of. Firstly, because many Roman Catholics make the assumption that true authority is vested in the Roman Catholic Church they also believe that anyone who opposes this is automatically wrong. Likewise they believe that their ordained priests are the only ones 'qualified' to be the intermediaries between men and God, therefore, anyone who disagrees with their priests must also be wrong. Ironically many Roman Catholics do not themselves agree with all that the Church teaches, however, they still make the assumption that the Roman Catholic Church, with its clergy, is the official voice of Christendom, and this mitigates against a questioning of what they have been taught. Secondly, many Roman Catholics enjoy the physicality of their faith and therefore struggle to comprehend the simplicity of the Gospel. To be a good Catholic one needs to go to confession, pray some set prayers and take the Eucharist. In this way salvation is earned. As the devotee goes through these ritualistic forms of his faith, he feels as if he is being proactive and really doing something good and positive. To be told that there is nothing he can do towards his salvation, that it is simply a matter of having faith in the finished work of Christ, is a huge hurdle to cross.

The biggest problem when witnessing to Roman Catholics, however, is apathy. The church provides for them a closed package. They find forgiveness and moral support from the Church and so they do not see the need to become 'born-again', especially when this message is preached by people about whom they are suspicious. There is good reason for their suspicion. From the Roman Catholic point of view Protestantism seems so divided. Whereas all Roman Catholics see themselves as belonging to one unified Church under the leadership of the Pope, they see in Protestantism a confusing myriad of different interest groups with a wide range of doctrinal positions and a plethora of leaders. In countries such as France, Italy and Spain, Protestant groups, especially those that are evangelical, are so small that they are easily branded as 'sects'. Compared to the Roman Catholic Church with its power, unity, pomp and ceremony, they appear to be no more than 'unofficial' expressions of Christianity. The message, however clearly stated, is often met with a derisive shrug.

The Orthodox Church

If the Roman Catholic Church is the dominant expression of Christianity within Western and Central Europe, the Orthodox Church is the dominant expression in much of Eastern Europe. The Orthodox Church numbers about 150 million which is roughly about 1 in every 6 'Christians'. It claims to be a family of self-governing churches as opposed to a centralised organisation with a single head. Each of these self-governing churches are headed up by a patriarch. The four ancient Patriarchates of Constantinople, Alexandria, Antioch and Jerusalem are considered the most significant because of the historical role they have played, and of these the Patriarch of Constantinople is called the Universal Patriarch as his position is one of special honour. In addition to these there are other autocephalous (with their own government and figure-head) churches in Russia, Romania, Serbia, Greece, Bulgaria, Georgia, Cyprus, Poland, Albania and Sinai.

The Orthodox Church attributes its origins to the

Emperor Constantine. Having won the Battle of Milvian Bridge, Constantine took control of the Roman Empire. In 313 AD he signed an Edict of Toleration which liberated Christianity from persecution, and then in 324 AD decided to move the capital of the Empire to Constantinople. This in time made Rome and Constantinople rival centres of Christianity, and following several theological and leadership debates, the Great Schism of 1054 AD separated the two churches forever.

Like the Roman Catholic Church, the Orthodox Church is steeped in tradition. Its three greatest sources of tradition are the Bible, the Seven Ecumenical Councils and the Creed. The Nicene-Constantinopolitan Creed is considered the most important of the ecumenical statements of faith. Unlike the Roman Catholic Church the Orthodox Church puts particular stress on icons as part of their tradition and believe that icons are one of the ways in which God is revealed to man.

Liturgy is extremely important to Orthodox believers and, like their Roman Catholic counterparts, they are committed to praying to the saints and for the dead. They do not believe in the infallibility of the Pope, but they do believe in the infallibility of the Church as it expresses itself through the ecumenical councils. They hold to seven sacraments (baptism, chrismation, the Eucharist, repentance/confession, holy orders, marriage and anointing of the sick). Of these baptism and the Eucharist have a special position.

Responding to Religious Europeans

How are we to witness to people who form part of religious

Europe? What do we say to people who are committed members of either the Roman Catholic or Orthodox Churches?

The first thing we need to do is to be cautious about our attitude. In my experience you do not get very far in evangelism by criticising or ridiculing another person's sincerely held belief-system. By that I am not suggesting that we should never confront people with the truth or dismantle the false worldview upon which they stand. Quite the reverse! But ultimately it is the Holy Spirit who convicts using the Word of God and this will always be more powerful than any criticism that I might launch at another person. While there will inevitably be discussions in any evangelistic situation about whose position is true, evangelism also involves loving and respecting those whom we want to reach. So we must endeavour to help them understand this because you can win an argument and yet lose the person. Only when the person we witness to is convinced of our love and care for them will they be willing to open up and listen to the truth. A belligerent and aggressive attitude will prove counterproductive.

I remember some years ago taking part in an evangelistic outreach in a small town in the Republic of Ireland. Much of the outreach involved door-to-door work, and as I went around knocking doors I noted that people were unusually hostile. I was alarmed by this because the Irish are well known for their friendliness and hospitality. On one particular doorstep I asked the man I was speaking to why he was so aggressive towards Evangelicals. He disappeared and came back with a Gospel tract that had been put through his letterbox the previous week. I quickly read the tract and everything became clear. It was written in a very aggressive and insulting style and was a deliberate attack on the Roman Catholic Church. While some of the points made were no doubt true, others were conjecture and had nothing to do with the presentation of the Gospel. Any sincere Roman Catholic reading the tract would have every right to be offended. Although the person who distributed these tracts throughout the town was doing so with good intentions, the impact had not been to open people's hearts to the Gospel but rather had turned them off evangelical Christianity. A wrong attitude in evangelism is a very dangerous thing.

Secondly we need to focus on the centrality of Scripture. My reason for saying this is twofold. Firstly, the vast majority of Roman Catholics and Orthodox Christians believe the Bible to be the inspired Word of God. We therefore have a basis for discussion because they respect the Bible and will be willing to consider its implications. In addition, we will have to confront the issue of Roman Catholic or Orthodox 'tradition' at some point in the evangelism process, precisely because this tradition is a barrier to true belief in Christ. However, the question will arise as to what authority we possess in questioning this body of tradition. Most Catholics that I have met see their Church as the official voice of Christianity, and their Orthodox counterparts feel similarly about their Church. Even those who have some sympathy towards Evangelical Christians nonetheless regard the Evangelical Church as an inferior Church compared to the officialdom of Rome or Constantinople. Indeed in many parts of Europe evangelicals are commonly branded as a 'sect' or 'cult' and have little by way of credibility. The only way to overcome this prejudice is to make Scripture central and call upon its authority in any discussion. In my experience few sincere Catholics or Orthodox Christians will deny the authority of the Bible even if they are not obeying it.

A third thing we need to do is to stick doggedly to the Bible's salvation storyline. This needs to be stressed because there is always the temptation to divert any conversation towards side issues which are of lesser consequence. In truth, if I am witnessing to a Roman Catholic there is no need to argue about how many sacraments there are, whether or not priests should be celibate or whether the church should be headed by a pope or not. What is relevant is that all have sinned, even those who are deeply religious, and because of sin all of mankind stands condemned. They need to know that we cannot merit salvation no matter how much religious ritual we go through. The only hope of salvation is faith in the finished work of Christ who died once and for all on the cross, and the only thing that we contribute to this process of salvation is the sin from which we are saved. Of course, all of this can be clearly demonstrated from the Bible. Where this conflicts with 'tradition' we simply need to stress that the Bible is the revealed will of God and therefore it must be obeyed.

I am not suggesting that this is a simple thing to do. Indeed in one conversation I had with an Italian Catholic last year I was reminded by him that the Church is the interpreter of truth. To him, even though the Bible appears to conflict with what he had been taught, this must not, in his understanding be a real conflict, because the priest knows best. This is a frustrating situation to be in, but the best thing to do is to stick to what the Bible says and pray that the Holy Spirit will use the Word of God to make its impact.

Similarities and differences

As we engage in dialogue with Religious Europeans we may well be faced with a number of challenges and questions that will impinge on our relationship with them. To begin with, both Roman Catholics and Orthodox adherants will see themselves as Christians. While their initial response towards us might be one of suspicion, as our relationship with them builds they will learn to appreciate us and recognise our commitment to God. The question then arises as to what differences there are between us. This in turn can lead to a number of practical issues.

We might be asked about our attitude to the Roman Catholic or Orthodox Churches and equally our attitude towards these Churches might be tested in some tangible way. On one occasion, for example, while I was doing a mission in Malta I was invited by a Roman Catholic charismatic group to join them for an open air worship service. The choruses being sung at this service were the same as the ones we sing at my church, and the liturgy, although distinctly Roman Catholic, nevertheless clearly exalted Christ. On another occasion I was invited by a Roman Catholic priest in Italy to join him in praying for the moral and spiritual needs of the nation. On yet another occasion I was asked by a Roman Catholic priest in the area where I lived to join him and several other priests in a national campaign on an important moral issue.

In each of these situations the invitations arose as a result of my attempts to get alongside Roman Catholics so that I could witness to them. The warmth of my relationship with these people, which was clearly a very positive thing, led to the situation where I had to make a choice. A great deal was at stake because there was the potential for offence being caused. These are not easy situations to deal with and there is no perfect formula which we can apply. However, as a general rule I would decline participating in something that clearly negates the power and truth of the Gospel, but am happy to participate in things that do not. Perhaps one further example would be helpful in clarifying this distinction.

I was once invited to join with some Roman Catholic friends as they participated in the mass at their local church. I would not have had a problem being an observer at the celebration, indeed I have done so on a number of occasions, but I would not actually be a participant at the mass because it contravenes the Gospel in its claim to be a sacrifice and to offer forgiveness for sin. On that occasion I thought it best to decline the invitation. However, I felt much more comfortable participating in the first three examples I mentioned. I did join in at the open air service in Malta and was able to share my faith with some of the worshippers afterwards. When I was invited by the Italian priest to pray with him I did so, and also prayed for him. This did not call into question my commitment to the Gospel, but it did give me the opportunity to share with him something of my love for God as evidenced in my prayers. I was also happy to join the ethical campaign which was being spearheaded by some Catholic priests as I believed that the issue we were fighting for was one which God had a concern about. Once again it did not negate my belief in the Gospel, but positively demonstrated my commitment as an Evangelical Christian to biblical values.

In describing these occasions I am not suggesting that all

Evangelicals should respond in the same way or that the decisions I took should be normative practice in our evangelism and relationship with Religious Europeans. My experience of evangelism has suggested that situations we find ourselves in are often complex and require a lot of thought and careful weighing up. It is therefore difficult to distil our approach to simple formulae.

However, I think there are two things that we have to keep in balance. Firstly, we need to ensure that we do nothing that detracts from our presentation of the Gospel. In the case of the mass that I was invited to, participation would have suggested an agreement with that practice which is clearly unbiblical, so it was not difficult to refuse. Secondly, we need to remember that Jesus mixed freely with people and spent time with them. He ate with the tax collectors and sinners, worshipped in the Temple, recognised the faith of the Gentile centurion and spoke to the woman at the well, all without sin. This kind of incarnated ministry should be our model and will require a commitment to get alongside people where they are and make the Christian faith real to them.

If we can keep this balance and use every opportunity to clearly communicate the truth of the Gospel, if we can articulate the difference between true Christianity and mere religion, then I believe we can effectively speak into the lives of even the most Religious Europeans. Of course, in all this we are dependent on the work of the Holy Spirit, who convicts people of sin and their need of a Saviour.

Chapter 5
Thinking about Enlightenment Europeans

Although Christianity (in its broadest sense) is still influential in Europe and finds expression through institutions such as the Roman Catholic and Orthodox Churches, it is nevertheless on the decline. While Religious Europeans are still numerous they are not the only people we need to think about. We now turn our focus to the Enlightenment Europeans, that is to those Europeans who believe truth can be discovered by human reasoning and choose not to align themselves with the Church or Christianity because they are profoundly sceptical of these sources of truth.

Enlightenment Europeans come in all sorts of shades from committed atheists to those who simply label themselves as agnostics or sceptics. Indeed many Enlightenment Europeans are regular church attendees. They have real doubts and questions about the existence of God, they are thoroughly sceptical, yet they continue to attend church as it is part of the habit of their lives. What cannot be doubted is that a great many Europeans fit into this category. Why are they so numerous? What has prompted so many people in a continent with such a long history of Christianity to reject Christian claims and opt for a more sceptical position?

Why do people question?

The answer to these questions is complex and would take many pages to properly explore. However a number of simple and obvious causes are worth mentioning. Firstly, there is the development of science which has significantly impacted our daily lives as well as our understanding of the universe. Scientific endeavour has led many to believe that ultimately all the answers will be found through science. No one is naïve enough to suggest that we have those answers yet, or that we have any definitive answers. But the sheer expansion of scientific knowledge over the past few centuries has given many a sense of confidence that man really is the master of his universe, and this in turn has negated the need for a personal God upon whom we rely. Not only has science developed, but along with this development a myth has arisen which suggests that somehow religious belief is the enemy of science and the two must inextricably be in conflict. This is not true, of course, but such popular notions are hard to dispel. The conclusion is often drawn that science deals with evidence and religion with belief (perhaps even superstitious belief) so the two cannot be reconciled to each other.

Secondly, enlightenment attitudes are fostered as a result of the erosion of confidence in Scripture. During the 19th century Germany was the breeding ground of what became known as Biblical criticism. Scholars began to ask questions about the authorship of different books of the Bible and when certain books were written. They came to the conclusion that many books of the Bible were not written by the people identified in the book, but by other people living in a different time period. They also suggested that some Biblical books were collections of writings compiled by editors who were not overly concerned with historical facts and events.

This process began to pour doubt on the historical reliability of the Bible and divested it of its supernatural content. Although these deliberations took place in universities, the ideas presented began to percolate down to ground level to the point where the average man in the street instinctively doubts the reliability of the Bible even though he has never read it. The established Church has played a role in this undermining of the Bible. I have met ministers and pastors who openly question the authority of Scripture and encourage their congregations to take a more cautious approach towards Biblical truth. With the erosion of confidence in the Bible, the door has become wide open for any sceptic to deny the authority of the Bible and feel that his position is intellectually credible.

A third significant issue which has promoted an enlightenment approach is the problem of suffering. The issue of suffering has been a thorny one for humankind since the Fall. Suffering has many causes – man's inhumanity to man, natural disasters and the ravages of disease. Not only do people experience suffering in their own lives, but our modern media age has brought the world's suffering into our living rooms. If famine strikes Ethiopia, a tsunami hits Sri Lanka, or AIDS wipes out another family in India we know all about it. The existence of all this suffering has caused many Europeans to question whether there is a God. After all, if there was such a being as God who was all-powerful, He could stop the suffering. If He was good He would want to stop suffering. But because there is so much suffering, God is either bad, weak, both, or He simply doesn't exist.

Each of the categories mentioned in this book are broad and this is no less so when it comes to Enlightenment Europeans. This category incorporates a wide range of opinions. The hard edge of this enlightenment thinking is atheism. From conviction atheists insist that God cannot exist, or at least His existence is highly improbable. Typical of this viewpoint is Richard Dawkins, Charles Simonyi Professor for the Understanding of Science at Oxford University. In best selling books such as the 'Blind Watchmaker' and the 'Selfish Gene' he sets out his philosophy dressed in scientific language.

Dawkins is utterly committed to the theory of evolution and he believes that all life and matter originated as a result of blind, purposeless forces. A view such as this leaves no room for a God who is creator, as the universe is a closed system. Evolution, of course, is not just a scientific theory. In its purest form it is also a philosophy or belief-system. Those who espouse evolution and take it to its logical conclusions also believe in naturalism, that is, they believe that everything that we see around us must have some naturalistic explanation. If all life originates as a result of a cosmic accident and was unplanned, then there is no room for the supernatural, no God, no creator, all that exists is nature. When thinking about the origin of life naturalists cannot leave themselves open to the possibility of a creator because he would be beyond nature. Moreover, when dealing with any issue or question, the answer must be based in nature, there must be a cause or reason that can be explicable in some naturalistic, observable way, and capable of scientific investigation.

Of course it would be inaccurate to say that everyone who believes in the theory of evolution is a naturalist. Indeed there are some very fine Christians who believe in God as creator yet hold to the theory of evolution. This position, however, is somewhat inconsistent and denies the philosophical under-girding of naturalism. In practice, the majority of people who understand evolution and believe it are philosophical naturalists and their worldview leaves little room for belief in God. They may claim to hold to a belief in a creator in tandem with a belief in evolution, but they have little by way of commitment to the former belief because in practice the latter nullifies it. God might not be dead, but He is squeezed into a corner and remains obsolete.

Atheists such as Dawkins are not very numerous in European society, but they are a sufficiently large group to merit attention, and their influence is significant in promoting secularism in European society. Most universities throughout Europe are thoroughly secular and their science departments are staffed with faculty committed to both evolution as a scientific theory and naturalism as a philosophy.

Learning to witness

How do we begin witnessing to those who claim to be atheists? What do we say to them when they tell us that they could never believe the Bible because it is no more than a book of superstitious myths? Ultimately, of course, we want to introduce them to the Bible and get them to read it for themselves. I have no doubt that if someone honestly approached the Bible with a desire to learn, God would speak to them despite their prejudices. However, if the Bible is totally disregarded because of their belief in naturalism, then we need an approach which will ultimately bring them to the recognition of the importance of the Bible.

In such circumstances, when the listener is blinded by his or her own philosophy, it is important to begin by exposing the weakness of their belief-system. In the case of most atheists this will involve raising serious questions about the origin of the universe and of life, and questioning the validity of evolution as science. Doing so might seem a difficult thing to do, especially if the person asking the question does not have a science background, and does not possess the philosophical apparatus to argue the case for theism in any convincing way. Atheists often accuse Christians of being anti-scientific because of their belief in God and this adds to the complexity of the issue. However, there are a number of points that can easily be made which provoke thought.

God doesn't hate science

The first thing that we need to acknowledge is that there is no intrinsic hostility between Christianity and science. Indeed, many of the founding fathers of science such as Leonardo Da Vinci, Blaise Pascal, Sir Isaac Newton,

Michael Faraday and William Thompson were Christians. Moreover for many of these men their study of science enhanced their faith because they were able to wonder at the greatness of God as seen through the complexity and beauty of His creation. Sir Isaac Newton is particularly interesting as he wrote more volumes on theology than he did on science.

The Religion of Evolution

Secondly, we need to point out that evolution is as much a belief-system as Christianity. In scientific investigation the scientist will look at all the available evidence and propose a theory which he feels provides the best explanation for the data. If the evidence is consistently found to justify the theory then it becomes more credulous and is believed as empirical fact (that is a belief that has been tested and approved). If, however, the case is not proven or disproved, the theory remains just that – a theory.

Though many people within the scientific and educational establishment claim that evolution is a fact, that it has been tested and proved to be true, this is simply not the case! At best, the jury is still out on the issue; at worst, evolution is an elaborate fabrication. Despite the efforts of such luminaries as Julian Huxley, Francis Crick and of course Richard Dawkins, the case has simply not been justified. Indeed there are many significant barriers which the theory needs to overcome before it can reasonably be accepted. There is the problem of the fossil record which strongly suggests that gradual mutation did not occur. There is the complexity of cell structures and especially DNA which defy any attempt to explain their existence on the basis of mere chance. There are the problems of how larger creatures were able to mutate and transform themselves into something quite different without becoming extinct in the process. Then there are questions about how to reconcile the theory of evolution with the law of thermodynamics. Added to this, and in the light of ongoing research, there is a growing number of scientists who simply do not accept evolution as a given[27].

All of this, of course, means that the theory of evolution is not in the realm of 'fact', rather, it is in the realm of belief. In that case it is the same as Christianity. The realm of science should not be separated radically from the realm of faith. In both cases the issues of probability and truth apply. As Christians we can therefore validly ask the atheists which is the more probable position: that there is an intelligent designer who made the universe, or that mindless and purposeless particles suddenly conspired to bring about existence from non-existence? We can also ask them why their faith statement should be accepted as truth, and give them reasons as to why Christianity should be accepted as truth.

Certainly the weaknesses in the theory of evolution raise real questions about the validity of atheism. Of course the scientific data available to us does not prove God's existence, but neither can it sustain any claim that God does not exist. This point needs to be made forcibly. Having pointed out the weaknesses in the evolutionary theory, we then need to demonstrate to the atheist that belief in God's existence is something which is both intellectually respectable and compelling. There are a number of simple ways of doing this.

I think a good starting point is to ask questions about why we, and the universe, exist. Our universe is remarkably complex and so are we. The very existence of all of this is indeed suggestive of a designer. If such a designer does indeed exist then why would He go to all the trouble to create a system so breathtaking in its intricacy and beauty, why create humans with their spiritual capacity, an instinctive desire to worship, and a moral conscience? Such questions lead naturally to the relationship between God and man and draw the listener to seek answers which can be found in the Bible. Furthermore when investigating the Bible itself one cannot help but be impressed by such phenomena as Biblical prophecy. It simply cannot be explained away without recognising the involvement of the supernatural.

This, however, is only half the battle. It seems to me that we should not only give sound intellectual reasons for believing in the existence of God, but we should also demonstrate that belief in God is actually a very attractive thing. Despite the technological advancement of our modern world, we nevertheless live in a society where loneliness, hopelessness and despair are commonplace. In extreme cases some Europeans commit suicide, not because they are poor, but because they feel life is simply not worth living. It is here that the Christian message can have a real impact. It is good news for those who feel oppressed. Jesus Christ offers us relief from guilt and a purpose in life. To know Jesus is to have something worth living for. He gives us meaning and significance in a world lacking purpose and hope. This point must be enthusiastically emphasised so that the atheist can see that Christianity is not only intellectually credible, but also desirable.

If we can get atheists to the point where they are willing to read the Bible objectively and openly, and are prepared to discuss the implications of the claims which the Bible makes on their lives, we will have accomplished a great deal. Coupled with prayer and an intelligent presentation of the Gospel, this will prove a potent witnessing strategy.

Dealing with Agnostics

Not all Enlightenment Europeans are atheists. Many people are sceptical about the Christian faith, not because they believe God does not exist, but because they have serious questions about faith. These questions may have no relationship to the question of whether or not God exists, rather they are of a more general nature.

For some there are questions about the reliability of the Bible. After all the Bible is a book written a very long time ago by people with whom we have no direct link. The original documents have long since been destroyed and so all we have now is copies of copies. How do we know that the Bible we have can be trusted? Others might question the reliability of some of the accounts written in the Bible. For example, how do we know that Jesus did in fact perform all the miracles that are attributed to him? There are still others who question whether the belief in God is consistent with the suffering in the world.

In truth the list of questions and doubts which people might have is almost endless. So how do we tackle them and effectively share the Gospel with them? The first thing we must do is take people's doubts seriously. This seems an obvious thing to say, but I have often been surprised by how glib some Christians can be about the doubts that their non-Christian friends have. I can remember once dealing with this issue at an evangelism seminar. One of the people at the seminar whom I knew to be an avid evangelist boldly stated that when non-Christians raise intellectual questions it is simply because they want to avoid the issue of their personal sin and their spiritual status before God. This is simply not true in the majority of cases. People genuinely do have doubts about Christianity and when they voice them it is often because they want to find the answer as they are genuinely interested. As one non-Christian once said to me, 'I would love to become a Christian, I just don't understand what it is all about'.

That people have doubts should not surprise us. As Christians we believe in a being (God) whom we cannot see, touch, smell or hear. We believe that salvation comes as a result of something that happened 2000 years ago and we claim that our sins are taken away through, what could appear to non-Christians, just a simple prayer. Moreover, we share this message with people who are spiritually blind though intellectually alive, people who have grown up in a secular culture that denies the spiritual and have gone through an education system that prizes rationality and empirical science. Where do we as Christians get our information about salvation from? It comes from copies of a book completed two millennia ago of which the original documents have long since disappeared. All of this gives good reason for the thinking person to ask searching questions, and if we really love people we should be willing to take their questions seriously.

A second thing we need to do with the sceptics to whom

we are witnessing is to encourage them to honestly and sincerely search the Bible to discover truth and to discover it in the Bible. If the early chapters of Hebrews teach us anything it is that God is a communicator and if we listen to what He is saying then our lives can be transformed. If someone is genuinely seeking, they can find the truth even if they have significant intellectual questions that need answering along the way.

Perhaps one of the best ways of encouraging people to seek truth is to demonstrate what is at stake. If someone goes into eternity without Christ they are utterly doomed and there is no second chance. They need to face these spiritual realities and not allow any other apparent priority to get in the way of trusting in Christ. This should be strongly impressed on the sceptic.

Chapter 6
Thinking about Emergent Europeans

The changes in European society that brought about the emergent generation are dramatic and far reaching. On one level European society appears to be improving. With the possible exception of the Balkan States and one or two other isolated pockets, Europe appears to be a continent at peace. Democracy has spread throughout the region and, in relative terms, Europe seems to be characterised by good governance. There is also a great deal of prosperity. True, this is unevenly distributed and unemployment and weak economies conspire to ensure that many Europeans are genuinely struggling. Overall, however, there is a prosperity throughout the continent that previous generations could only have dreamed of. Europe is also more integrated and educated than at any time in its history.

What must be recognised, however, is that when Europe is viewed from a spiritual point of view the situation is more gloomy by far. We have already touched upon the residual influence of medieval thinking on modern day Europe. We have also noted that Europe has its fair share of enlightenment sceptics. Both of these groups are a challenge to anyone who wishes to proclaim the Gospel. But the emergent generation provides for us no less a challenge, not least because, as I stated in chapter 1, this emergent generation has become the most culturally dominant in Europe today.

A questioning of truth

What then is the emergent generation? What do they believe and how do they function? How do we define an Emergent European? The very first characteristic of Emergent Europeans is their questioning of absolute truth. Previous generations of Europeans believed that truth existed in an absolute sense and could be acquired. The way in which it was acquired varied. For Medieval Europeans truth came from God via the Church, in enlightenment times truth could be discovered through human reason and logic. Different pathways but both, it was accepted, led to truth in an absolute and culturally transcending way. For Emergent Europeans, however, truth is an entirely personal thing and should not be seen as objective.

Emergent Europeans recognise the role the Church has played in society and do not doubt that good things have been done by the Church in the past. However, they are also aware of the bad that has been done and have a tendency to see Christian belief as somewhat dogmatic and intolerant. Likewise they see the value of science, but recognise that science has also brought industrial pollution, gross inequality and nuclear weaponry. It has benefits, but flaws also. The result has been that for Emergent Europeans neither Christianity nor science have the capability of solving all man's problems. Both contain truth, but their truths are not absolute, just personal truths in a world of diverse truths.

This process of denuding the word truth of any objective content has been greatly speeded up by the advent of the global village and mass media. People in the West are now continually bombarded with the cultures and value systems of peoples from all over the world. These have inevitably been compared to Western culture and values, and in many cases Western culture has been found wanting. Increasingly we are developing an eclectic culture where any value or idea can easily be assimilated. What was once considered to be true, correct and normative is now not seen in this way. It is not so much that truth has been challenged, but the definition of truth has changed altogether. Truth is merely a matter of opinion not an expression of what is real and actual.

Downgrading of deity

Another feature of Emergent Europeans is that God has ceased to be central in their thinking. In one sense this is not a new phenomenon. The Enlightenment and the modernist culture which it spawned also questioned God. The theory of evolution, developed by Charles Darwin, provided the sceptics with a naturalistic explanation for the universe which removed any necessity for God. It made atheism intellectually satisfying and enabled science to take the position now understood to be vacated by God.

The difference in the way God is viewed by Emergent Europeans is that God is not opposed; He is merely downgraded to a position of anonymity. In today's society you will find few people who argue aggressively that God does not exist. Those who do are seen to fit into an Enlightenment bracket which is rather aloof, bookish and dated. However, God has been so devalued in most people's eyes that He is simply not worth arguing over. It matters little, therefore, what view a person has about the existence of God, it will merely be interpreted as his opinion and not some objective reality with which everyone must acquiesce. He is not the transcendent God of the universe, rather He is a hobby, somewhat like football or tennis. If you are into that kind of thing that's good, but you should not expect everyone to do the same.

It is interesting to note that many Emergent Europeans do not reject spirituality. Indeed, tarot cards, crystals and the reading of star signs is as popular as ever. If a fortune-teller sets up her stall and offers to reveal the mysteries of life there will be a huge queue of people wanting to listen. People are also drawn to the kind of mass spirituality which was seen in events such as the funeral of Princess Diana [13]. The difference is that these forms of spirituality are not sustained by any concept of objective truth. Indeed it does not really matter to participants whether what they are doing is logical or based on some kind of proven Biblical revelation. Rather, they are subjective, experience-orientated spiritualities that have no respect for what actually is.

Relativised morality

The questioning of absolutes has also led to a moral

framework that has been relativised to the point where it has become meaningless. Among Emergent Europeans a thing can no longer be considered to be right or wrong in a moral sense. Rather, the talk is of lifestyle choices. If someone chooses to live as a homosexual, smoke dope or use foul language, we cannot condemn him, there being no moral yardstick by which his actions can be judged. If objections are raised, the person objecting will be dismissed as an intolerant bigot. Emergent Europe has essentially abolished sin.

The media propagates this new moral freedom by handing over the responsibility for this to the audience who then decide how morals are constructed. Today's arbiters of morality are the talk show hosts who canvas public opinion and determine what is right. Even news bulletins are punctuated with opinion polls which ask the audience to text in and determine whether something is right or wrong, good or bad. Decisions made are not determined by any objective moral code, but by the personal taste of the individual or group. In practice this means that morality is reduced to its lowest common denominator. I will not vote against anything that I myself might at some point want to do. Consequently as long as no one is hurt and mother nature is undamaged, anything goes.

Pluralism

What is true for morals within Emergent Europe is also true when it comes to religion. The lack of absolutes means that no one faith can claim to be true in an absolute sense. At best a particular faith can be no more than true for the individual. Though the West is considered to be at least nominally Christian, the reality is that Christianity occupies no more space on the shelves of the spiritual supermarket than any other religion. All religions are considered equal, and equally true. Perhaps this can be most clearly seen in the way religion is taught in schools. No special place is given to Christianity and children are taught to respect all religious traditions equally. Each religion is seen as valid for those who are practitioners.

In such a society the only heresy that exists is the suggestion that what someone else believes might actually be wrong. Evangelism, therefore, is by its very nature an abhorrent practice as it presupposes that what another person believes is in some way inadequate. The average man in the street is quite happy for a Christian to have beliefs provided he doesn't expect others to become believers. Any attempt to convince someone of the rightness of Christianity will be met with questions about why Christianity is any different from any other faith.

The net result of this is that in much of European society the Bible carries no authority. Because of the nominal Christian heritage that most Europeans have, they would recognise what the Bible is and might even recognise terms like 'the Word of God' when used in reference to it. However, most Europeans, especially the Emergents, would be at least slightly sceptical of it and a great many when pushed would not be able to articulate whether or not they see the Bible as being essentially different from the Koran or the Bhagavad-Gita. Certainly most would not see it as an authoritative guide to their faith and practice and only a fraction of Europeans would have ever read a single

Bible book through, let alone the whole Bible. It is just one among many religious works.

Experience

A further trait among Emergent Europeans is their obsession with experience. Facts have been replaced by feelings and truth by experience. I have already mentioned Nietzsche's belief that an idea need not be true as long as it is 'life-affirming'. That is, if it gives the person a feeling of strength and freedom then it is of no consequence whether the idea is objectively true. The contemporary maxim, 'If it feels good do it', says more or less the same thing. Life is not built on objective truths but on experiences; actions should be judged, not by any moral yardstick, but by whether we enjoy the experience of living.

This desire for experience can be seen throughout the continent. It can be seen in the many beautiful shopping centres where the experience of shopping is as important as obtaining the goods. It can be seen in a culture where buying things for their usefulness is less important than the image and identity which the commodity can provide or the retail therapy itself. It can be seen in the diversity of music and the multi-channel digital revolution. It can also be seen in politics where image and sound-bite is a more potent vote winner than substance and policy[28].

In short, Emergent Europe is a society where God is irrelevant; where Scripture carries no weight; where people are confused with a mass of religious options all of which are considered to be equally valid and where there is no sin except that of believing something to be absolutely true.

Witnessing to Emergent Europeans

Having thought about some of the presuppositions that govern Emergent Europeans we must think once again of how we witness to this particular group of Europeans. My personal conviction and experience is that this is the hardest group of people to impact. The reason for this is that there is a great deal of work that has to be done even before we can get down to discussions on the truthfulness and coherence of the Christian worldview. This is because Emergent Europeans struggle with the concept of truth in the first place. When dealing with Religious Europeans we can easily discuss the contrast between religious tradition and the Bible, and when dealing with Enlightenment Europeans we can have fruitful discussions on the origin of life and the limitation of Darwinian evolution. Even when dealing with Europeans from other religious persuasions we can discuss the merits of Christ and the Bible because they have a belief in religious truthfulness. However, when we turn to Emergent Europeans we discover that they only believe in truth for the individual. Therefore, our starting point with them must be about the issue of truth itself and its objective reality.

What is Truth?

Dealing with the concept of truth in evangelism is of utmost importance. After all the Gospel is not good news merely because it is a nice story, rather it is good news because it is true. We need, therefore, to demonstrate that truth is a real concept and that Christianity can be seen to be true. This will not always be easy for two reasons. Firstly, as we have seen from chapter one, truth has been seen in different ways and secondly, because truth is actually a difficult notion to understand[29]. It cannot just be reduced to as simple a formula as 'something which can be logically and scientifically proved'. For example, it is true that I love my wife, but I cannot think of a mathematical equation or scientific experiment which could demonstrate this truth. Despite this, however, there is a rational aspect to truth. This rational aspect does not actually create truth, rather it tests it. It asks the question, 'Is there any evidence to support the truth in which I believe?' Given this, perhaps we can come up with a simple (maybe simplistic) definition of truth. Truth could be described as a belief which can be validated[30]. Later when this is applied to Christianity we will be able to demonstrate not only that truth exists, but Christianity can be demonstrated to be the truth.

Critiquing Pluralism

Having demonstrated that truth can indeed exist in an absolute sense, we then need to remove any philosophical barriers that might prevent emergent thinkers from believing in Christ. This is an obvious step because even if a person does admit that something can be true it does not follow that they will automatically believe that the truth is embodied in the Christian Gospel. After all there will be so many other religious options to consider.

Removing these philosophical barriers is, of course, only the beginning. Even if someone were to stand on a level playing field where he believed that Christianity it true, he would not necessarily become a Christian. Indeed it is probable that a great many people come to believe in the essential truthfulness of the Christian Gospel and yet do not go on to trust Christ. What is needed is the conviction of sin which the Holy Spirit alone can bring. Only when this occurs and a person is drawn to Christ will they believe. However the removal of these barriers is an essential starting point because a person will not become a Christian if he believes that there are genuine reasons for not accepting Christ.

The primary issue that we need to deal with at this point is that of pluralism. In essence pluralism is the belief that all religions lead to God and are of equal truthfulness and value. As we have already noted pluralism is one of the key traits of Emergent Europeans. The reason why we focus in on pluralism is that it questions Christianity's uniqueness and gives the non-Christian no reason to believe in Jesus as opposed to any other option. So how do we critique pluralism and demonstrate its falseness?

Firstly, we need to point out the weaknesses in the arguments for pluralism. We can begin this by noting that most religious pluralists argue that religious beliefs are culturally conditioned. In other words a Pakistani Muslim believes what he does because he comes from Pakistan and an American Christian believes what he does because he comes from the USA. They then go on to argue that as their beliefs are due solely to their background, and therefore not a conscious choice, we must accept that their 'truth' is true for them as opposed to universal truth. This means we must also accept it as a universally valid way of life, because it is 'true for them'.

This argument is actually nonsensical if carried to its logical conclusion. The implication of this line of reason would make Nazism, cannibalism, infanticide, suicide bombing and witchcraft both true and acceptable on the basis of being a result of geographic and cultural conditioning. This is a very obvious fault and to validate a belief simply because someone was inculcated in that belief from birth opens the floodgates for the acceptance of almost anything.

Secondly, we need to point out that religious pluralism is inherently unworkable because the religious pluralist cannot have his cake and eat it. What the religious pluralist is doing is to say that there is no such thing as absolute truth, and therefore, no one religion can claim to be true in an absolute and exclusive way. But the statement, '*there is no such thing as an absolute truth*', is in fact a statement which purports to be an absolute truth. It makes the religious pluralist intellectually arrogant because he denies anyone else the possibility of being right while claiming to be right himself; but more than that, he is denying the veracity of his own statement by his own statement. This is a truly ludicrous position[31].

Thirdly, religious pluralists are inconsistent in their application of their own principles. This is because although they claim that all religions are true and should be accepted as such, they do not actually believe this in a universal way. Indeed, every religious pluralist will contend against aspects of the belief-system of any faith[32]. For example someone might accept the truthfulness of Christianity and yet deny the uniqueness of Christ as the only Saviour of the world. The uniqueness of Christ is, of course, an essential feature of Christian belief, so clearly to deny this would be deeply inconsistent with the belief of the truthfulness of Christianity.

Reasonable stupidity

Having pointed out the weakness of pluralism as a philosophical concept, we then need to persuade those to whom we are witnessing to make a clear choice. I believe this can be done by demonstrating that two beliefs cannot both be true if they are contradictory, and that this very situation compels us to make a choice for one position or the other. I will illustrate this with a simple analogy.

Suppose I were sitting before an audience in an art class giving a lecture on the use of colour. As an illustration, I bring two large pieces of card with me and I hold them up. The card in my right hand is bright red, while the card in my left hand is green. As I deliver the lecture, I suddenly make the claim that the two pieces of card are actually the same colour. The class is surprised, and no wonder! They know that the card I am holding in my right hand is red. That is indisputable, because for all of their lives that particular colour has been labelled as red. The card in my left hand, however, is very different – it is green. At this point they all wonder why their lecturer has taken leave of his senses in claming that these two cards, which are clearly very different, are in fact the same colour. I try to reassure them by stating that it would be 'politically correct' to claim that the two cards are the same colour. After all in the emergent generation there are no absolutes and so my statement should not deserve contradiction. In any case, to accept my proposition the students would be able to demonstrate just how tolerant they are and in today's culture tolerance is highly prized. Despite my protests, the class simply cannot accept that two colours that are clearly different can actually be the same colour. It is simply illogical!

Much the same logic can be applied to how we view different religions. It is an absurdity to claim that they are all basically the same thing, however attractive such a position appears to be. The reality is that every religion claims that it is true, and true in an objective sense. As Ravi Zacharias states, 'At the heart of every religion is an uncompromising commitment to a particular way of defining who god is or is not and accordingly, of defining life's purpose'[33]. Not only do all religions stake their claim to truthfulness but they also differ from each other radically and irreconcilably. Any supposed similarities are small and relatively insignificant. To illustrate this point we will take a brief look at the comparison between Christianity, Hinduism, Buddhism, Shintoism and Islam.

Between them these faiths attract the loyalty of well over half of the world's population. They are, therefore, an excellent representative sample of world belief systems. When viewed carefully their differences are so great that they cannot find common ground even in their definition of who God is. Muslims are monotheists, people who see God as a single entity. Christians on the other hand, while believing in only one God, see Him in the three persons of the Father, Son and Holy Spirit. Hindus meanwhile cannot even agree among themselves as to what they believe about God. Some believe in one god, others in millions of gods, while others hold to a pantheistic belief that everything is god. Buddhism, on the other hand, is a non-theistic religion.

Likewise, when it comes to defining the nature of the human predicament, further disagreements emerge[34].

Hinduism, like its twin sister Buddhism, believes that humans are trapped within the cycle of rebirth (samsara) through which one transmigrates in accordance with the laws of karma. Shinto, on the other hand, does not have a strong sense of the fallenness of humanity; there is merely an imbalance. Islam does have an understanding of sin, but it is not as clear as the Christian understanding. There is no sense of the depravity of man and his bondage to sin; rather it is merely a weakness. These differences continue when it comes to the question of what salvation is[35]. For the Hindu, salvation is liberation from reincarnation, for the Buddhist it is the complete elimination of desire and the conditions for rebirth. In Shinto, salvation is achieving a healthy and robust life in the present, and for the Muslim, salvation is a future reality when Allah grants entry into paradise.

Even when apparent common ground is found, the wrangling continues. An example of this relates to the person of Jesus Christ in Islamic and Christian thought. Both Muslims and Christians have a belief system that includes Jesus. However, for the Christian, Jesus is the author of salvation whereas the Muslims recognise him merely as a great prophet. For Christians he is the incarnate Son of God, a point which the Muslim claims is blasphemous[36]. When it comes to the great work of Christ on the cross, another major division emerges. Christians are committed to a belief in the resurrection as an historical event, Muslims utterly reject that Jesus died[37].

It is interesting to note that Jesus said things during his ministry that clearly separated him from other world faiths. For example, he stated that God is the author of life and that if people wanted meaning and purpose in life they should come to him and find life. This is diametrically opposed to Buddhism, which is a non-theistic if not atheistic religion[38]. Jesus also claimed to be the Son of God and stated that if anyone saw him they were seeing God. Such a claim would be outrageous to a Muslim who, being a monotheist, would have no concept of God having a son or an equal. Jesus claimed to be the one who gives resurrection and eternal life, a concept very different from the Hindu idea of reincarnation. He also claimed that we could know God personally and that he would make the link between us and God, a point that an agnostic would find offensive because he would believe that God is unknowable. In all these ways Jesus drew a sharp distinction between his disciples and other world religions. We, therefore, do not have the luxury of saying that all religions are basically the same.

Sincerity does not make something true

When faced with this harsh reality, many Emergent Europeans will say, 'But what happens if these people from other religions are sincere, surely God would not condemn a sincere person'. This is such an emotive issue that even discussing it can elicit a hostile reaction, for after all, if people are sincere about something, surely that belief must be respected as true. This, of course, does not follow.

Centuries ago the Flat Earth Society came into being. The members of this society were committed to the belief that the earth was flat and not round. Subsequently modern science has proved beyond all reasonable doubt that the world is a globe, not flat, yet ironically the Flat Earth

Society still exists. It is not that evidence for the shape of the world is scant and dubious; on the contrary, it is overwhelming. Despite this, however, the society persists and its members sincerely believe that the earth is flat. Frankly it is ridiculous to accept the beliefs of the Flat Earth Society simply because they are sincerely held. The fact is they are wrong and sincerity is not an issue.

By the same token, religious sincerity is not an arbiter of truth. We should not judge the truthfulness of a religious claim simply because some people are deeply committed to it. Given that religion deals with the issue of man's eternal destiny, this issue is consequently of far more importance to us than the shape of the earth. We should never allow sentimentality and political correctness to damn mankind to a lost eternity just because they were not aware of what the truth was.

Having demonstrated that pluralism is an intellectually bankrupt way to view religious belief, we are now in a position to present to those to whom we are witnessing the truthfulness of Christianity. This needs to be done in two ways. Firstly, we need to defend the Bible as the revelation of God's truth, and secondly, we need to focus our hearer's attention on the person of Jesus Christ.

An Inspired Book

The reason we need to begin with a defence of the Bible is that what we believe about Jesus is found in the Bible, so if it can be demonstrated to be true, we will have a platform from which to declare the uniqueness of Christ. Our starting point in defending the Bible is the issue of inspiration. In 2 Timothy 3:16 we read, 'All scripture is inspired'[39]. This means that God through His Holy Spirit was involved in the writing process. What we have on the page are not just the thoughts of some human author, but of God Himself. No less a figure than Jesus himself ascribed authority to the Bible and demanded that we take it seriously. Of course, it does not necessarily follow that just because the Bible claims to be the inspired Word of God then it must be. Nevertheless the Bible's own understanding of itself brings us to the point where this claim needs to be investigated.

The Reality of Prophecy

Having begun with the issue of inspiration we then need to look for clues that suggest that God's hand was involved in the production of the Bible. Perhaps the most obvious clue is that of Biblical prophecy. Of course history has been full of prophets such as the secular prophet Nostradamus or the religious prophet Charles Taze Russell. However, on closer investigation, the prophecies made by these people have proved to be utterly unimpressive either because they were so ambiguous or because they simply did not come true. Biblical prophecies on the other hand are very impressive because they are specific and they have also been fulfilled exactly as the prophets foretold.

A good example of this is the prophecies made in the Old Testament about the coming of Jesus as Messiah. In total some 61 Messianic prophecies were made in the Old Testament predicting where Jesus would be born and how he would die and all of them were fulfilled by Jesus[40]. They make an overwhelming case for seeing the Bible as the unique Word of God.

Texts

Even given this compelling evidence some might still have serious doubts about the veracity of the Bible. In my experience two questions have most often been put to me. Firstly, I have been asked if I can be sure the Bible contains the same content as the documents that were originally penned, after all, none of the original documents (known as autographs) exist today. Secondly, I have been asked whether we can be sure that the Biblical writers really saw all that they claimed to see. This is a huge and complex issue, but we nevertheless have good reason for accepting that the documents we have are a reliable record of what took place.

Eye Witness Test

This confidence can be established if we apply to the Bible the same kinds of tests that scholars of antiquity apply to any ancient document. The first test scholars apply is called the 'eye witness test'. They are really asking what evidence exists to suggest that the writers of a document actually saw what they claimed. The Bible stands up very well to this test. Of course much of the Old Testament does not require this test because books like Proverbs, Psalms and Ecclesiastes are not histories. However, the sections that do require eye witness evidence have it in abundance. The Pentateuch, for example, which contains the first five books of the Bible, was written by Moses who was personally involved in many of the key events that took place. Likewise the New Testament shows a great deal of eye witness evidence. In Luke 1:1-4, for example, the writer tells us that he had carefully recorded what was said to him by eye-witnesses. His very style is suggestive of a careful researcher and he undoubtedly gleaned his information from the many eye-witnesses who were at the scene.

It is important to note the context within which Christianity emerged. Historians universally acknowledge that Christianity emerged in Jerusalem very shortly after the death and resurrection of Jesus Christ. It is clear from Acts chapter 2 that the Christians openly proclaimed their beliefs in the public arena and in the presence of both friendly and hostile witnesses. They even proclaimed both controversial and verifiable doctrines like the resurrection of Jesus. The Gospels were also circulated in the context of hostile witnesses, many of whom would have been around when the events recorded in them took place. Yet despite all of this we find no one refuting any of the claims in the Gospels with any plausibility. This strongly suggests that the Gospel writers knew what they were talking about, because they were actually there.

The Internal Test

A second test, the internal test, establishes the accuracy of the copies made and once again the Bible does very well. We know the Old Testament texts were copied accurately because of the reliability of the copying method. Copies of the Old Testament were produced by teams of dedicated copyists such as the Masorites. They produced exact copies of older documents in a systematic way. For example, once one page was copied from the original, every line on the page was counted and compared to the original to ensure that the copy had the same number of lines as the original. The same thing was done with the words and even the letters. There had to be the same number of letters on the copy as there was on the original, and the middle letter even had to be the same on the copy as it was in the original. If mistakes were found, the copy was promptly destroyed. This process appears obsessively strict, nevertheless it gives us excellent assurance of the reliability of the copying techniques.

Not only do these copying techniques give us a sense of confidence in the reliability of our Old Testament text, we also have ancient manuscripts which give us an objective test-case. The most famous of these are the Dead Sea Scrolls. The basis for the present text of the Hebrew Bible is the Masoretic Text, and this is the prototype against which all other texts are compared. The Dead Sea Scrolls were discovered by an Arab boy in 1947 and they contained 200 Biblical texts. The great significance of these scrolls is that they are 1,000 years older than the Masoretic Text and were dated only 300 years after the close of the Old Testament canon. When the two texts were examined together, it was discovered that there was very little change. That means that over this 1,000 year gap the copying techniques had proved reliable beyond all reasonable doubt.

When it comes to the New Testament, we can feel an equal confidence about its textual transmission, not least because of the sheer volume of New Testament documents in existence. There are some 25,000 manuscript copies of portions of the New Testament, far more than for any other document of the ancient world[41]. Not only is this impressive, but their close chronological proximity to the original manuscripts (autographs) is also impressive.

This point can easily be made when we compare the New Testament with the writings of Caesar, Plato and Homer. There are only 10 copies of the writings of Caesar in existence, 7 of Plato. While Homer does a little better with 643 copies, he is a long way behind the New Testament and its 25,000 copies. The earliest fragment of a New Testament document that we have dates back to about 114 AD, with the earliest books dating to 200 AD[42]. That means that there is a time span of only about 100 years between the original document and the earliest copy. The earliest copy of the works of Caesar dates from around 900 AD, the earliest copy of the works of Plato dates from 900 AD, while the earliest copy of Homer's Iliad dates from 400 BC. That means that the time distance between the original and the earliest surviving manuscript is about 1,000 years for Caesar, 1,300 years for Plato and 400 years for Homer.

DOCUMENT	No. Copies	Earliest Copy	Time Span
New Testament	25,000	200 AD (114 AD Fr.)	100 years
Caesar	10	900 AD	1000 years
Plato	7	900 AD	1300 years
Homer	643	400 BC	400 years

A Comparison of different historic documents.

No credible historian would doubt the existence of Caesar, Plato or Homer, and neither would they question the general reliability of what they wrote. That being the case, to question the reliability of the New Testament would be foolish[43]. The question that still remains, however, is how we know that what we have today still corresponds to what was written in the original manuscripts (autographs)? After all, however impressive this collection of documents may be, it does not in itself prove that the copying process which produced all these manuscripts is actually accurate. So how do we test the reliability of these New Testament manuscripts?

The answer to this question is actually very simple. As the New Testament was being copied the Church was spreading. Consequently new copying communities would appear in new areas. The key to testing the reliability of the copying process is to go as far back in the process as possible. If evidence of an early text can be found and compared to a more modern text, the extent of the reliability of transmission can be easily established. After all, the earlier a manuscript, the more likely it is to be accurate. But how do we find evidence of earlier texts? The key here is to compare distant relatives.

If several manuscripts were to be found in a single location, for example Alexandria, they could be compared to each other to see if they are similar. However, it is highly probable that they were all copied from the same manuscript. However, if one manuscript came from Alexandria, and another was taken from Rome, or Constantinople, or London, and compared, this would be more valid proof because the only connection between them would be a very early manuscript. Any similarity would therefore be proof of reliable transmission.

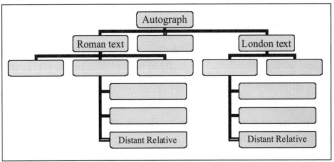

```
                    ┌──────────────┐
                    │  Autograph   │
                    └──────────────┘
       ┌───────────────────┼──────────────────────┐
  ┌──────────┐       ┌──────────┐           ┌──────────────┐
  │ Roman text│      │          │           │ London text  │
  └──────────┘       └──────────┘           └──────────────┘
 ┌────┬──────┬──────┐                      ┌──────────┬──────────┐
 │    │      │      │                      │          │          │
```

Comparing distant relatives to find the source.

Precisely this kind of test has been conducted with a great many sets of manuscripts and has given us great confidence in the integrity of the present New Testament text.

The External Test

There is one more test that scholars apply and that relates to external confirmation of the contents of the document? Once again the Old Testament does very well. For example, archaeologists have come up with an almost endless list of finds that have been able to confirm the Old Testament record in numerous ways. Indeed Donald Wiseman, Emeritus Professor of Assyriology in the University of London, states that some 25,000 sites relating to Biblical times have been uncovered[44]. None of these has in any way brought into question the events, places or people mentioned in the Old Testament.

The New Testament also passes the external test with flying colours. In the New Testament we have numerous references to people, places and events, all of which we can then look for in other historic documents.

The writings of Jewish historian Josephus are a good place to start. He mentions numerous people and places found within the New Testament and also tells us about the trial and death of Jesus as well as the continuation of Christianity. The former Rylands Professor of Biblical Criticism and Exegesis, F.F. Bruce states, *'Here, in the pages of Josephus, we meet many figures who are well known to us from the New Testament: the colourful family of the Herods; the Roman emperors Augustus, Tiberius, Claudius and Nero: Quirinias, the governor of Syria; Pilate, Felix and Festus, the procurators of Judea; the high-priestly families-Annas, Caiaphas, Ananias, and the rest; the Pharisees and the Sadducees; and so on. Against the background which Josephus provides we can read the New Testament with greater understanding and interest'*[45].

There are many other writings, besides those of Josephus, that we can turn to for information. Between the years of 70 AD and 200 AD the rabbis were referred to as the Tanna'im (repeaters of tradition). From this period there emerged a tradition known as the Baraitha. This was material external to the Mishnah but preserved by the Gemara. In the Baraitha we read about Jesus and the controversy which he caused within the Jewish establishment. It even tells us that Jesus was crucified on the eve of the Passover, which is exactly what John's Gospel tells us[46]. Further external evidence can be found among the pagan writers, the Apocryphal and miscellaneous works such as the Gospel of St. Thomas.

All this compelling evidence led Sir Fredrick Kenyon, formerly Principal Librarian and Director of the British Museum, a distinguished classical scholar, to write:

'The Christian can take the whole Bible in his hand and say without fear or hesitation that he holds in it the true Word of God, handed down without essential loss from generation to generation throughout the centuries'[47].

These tests when rigorously applied add credence to the Bible's claim to be the Word of God. Here is a book whose content is remarkable and life changing, but it is also a historical document based largely on the eyewitness accounts of honest men and women, some of whom died for their belief of the truthfulness of its contents. It is a book that has come under the scrutiny of rigorous scholarship and has been found to be a carefully preserved body of truth – such a book must be taken seriously as the Word of God.

What about other holy works?

Even after defending the Bible we may still be asked about other sacred texts. For many Emergent Europeans the Bible is just another religious book, no different from the Koran or the Bhagavad-Gita, so why do Christians believe that the Bible is the Word of God in an exclusive way?

This question can be answered by stating that the Bible has already made its case. It has an excellent pedigree and good reason to be accepted as the truth. Any other book which claims to be the Word of God must have the same credibility attached to its claims as the Bible does. It is not enough that another scripture appears to be good, helpful, or even revered by many. Any rival work must demonstrate clear justification for its claim to be the Word of God.

It must have the endorsement of a unique individual such as Jesus who not only declared the Bible to be authoritative, but lived up to the standards contained in it. It must be able to demonstrate an exceptional quality such as containing numerous prophesies that are then fulfilled, and it must be consistent throughout. In addition, it must have a transformative power that can not only affect the individual, but entire civilizations, and it must be confirmed by historical and archaeological evidence. Any rival work that does not match up to this list of criteria fails, whereas the Bible has achieved this list in every part.

Once you have the standard work, there is no need for lesser ones. The Bible is unique among the world's religious scriptures. It deserves to be accepted as the Word of God, a position which automatically denies recognition to any other religious work.

The Transcendent Christ

After defending the Bible we need to focus on the person of Jesus Christ. This is essential not only because he is the Saviour of the World, but because it is Christ that makes Christianity unique, he is its central figure.

Because the groundwork has already been done, this stage in the evangelism process is much less complicated than one would imagine. Once someone recognises that only one faith can credibly be true and that it is revealed to us in the pages of the Bible, the person of Christ is so compelling he can be seen to be in an utterly different realm than any other religious founder. Consequently, having shown the attractiveness of Christ, demonstrating reasons for believing in him becomes a relatively easy task. The problem, of course, is that 'men love darkness rather than light', so we still have a battle on our hands. Only through the power of the Holy Spirit can this battle ever be won. That having been said, the uniqueness and transcendence of Christ above all other founders of world religions is transparent and obvious.

Virgin birth

The very first thing about Jesus that we need to point out is that he is unique because he came into the world by miraculous means. He, unlike any other person who has ever lived, was born of a virgin. Of course, the doctrine of the virgin birth has been doubted by some, but any such doubts can quickly be dispelled under close investigation. The truth is that Mary and Joseph could have gained nothing from their claim that the baby Jesus was not actually Joseph's son. The 'scandal' was a terrible burden to bear, and not one that they would have willingly endured except for the fact that they knew that his conception was miraculous. He was conceived as a result of the activity of the Holy Spirit. This is the only credible explanation for their actions. That makes Jesus unique, for Mohammed, Krishna and Buddha all came into the world as a result of a conventional and ordinary birth, one in which nothing miraculous occurred.

Moral Purity

Secondly, Jesus is unique because he lived a life of utter moral purity. During his lifetime his adversaries continually tried to trip him up to find a way of accusing him. They followed him around the country trying to find fault, but their efforts were always in vain. Even at his trial under close investigation, the judge stated that no basis could be found for any kind of accusation. Clearly Jesus was a man who was utterly morally perfect.

The same could not be said of Mohammed, Buddha or even Krishna[48]. Indeed, their own scriptures admit to this. In the Koran we are told that Mohammed had to ask for forgiveness for his sin or face death. The Bhagavad-Gita has lurid descriptions of the immoral life that was lived by Krishna as he fraternised with the milkmaids. As for the Buddha, the very fact that he had to go through so many reincarnations presupposes sinfulness, for this process of rebirth purifies the individual. In each case the lives of these founders of world religions were flawed. Interestingly, the adherents of these faiths claim that their founders are able to empathise with ordinary people precisely because they are flawed characters. In this regard Jesus is unique because he led a life of purity that no one could question, and his utter holiness is attested throughout the Bible.

Proven Miracles

Thirdly, we need to point out that Jesus is unique because he performed many miracles that can be historically attested. Again there are those who doubt the veracity of the miracles of Jesus, but when their objections are put under the spotlight they are found to be unreasonable. There are many compelling reasons why we should believe in the historicity of the miracles of Jesus, but here we will mention just two[49]:

Firstly, the miracles of Jesus were done in a public setting and in the presence of hostile witnesses. Consequently many of those who watched these miracles taking place were not people with open minds, ready to accept and believe. Rather they were bitter cynics, desperate for the opportunity to humiliate Jesus and show him to be a fraud. Moreover some of Jesus' audience came from a conservative theological tradition whereby they firmly believed that miracles were by definition impossible. Despite their opposition, these sceptics simply could not deny miracles had taken place.

Secondly, some of Jesus' miracles were openly attested to after the event. The healings, for example, were proved to be valid by the continuing health of those who had been healed. If we were to go back to the first century we would have a hard job convincing Lazarus that the miracle that brought him back from the dead was in fact bogus!

The historically attestable nature of Jesus' miracles makes him unique, for no other religious founder performed miracles that can be historically attested as Jesus' miracles can[50].

Claimed Deity

Fourthly, Jesus is unique among the founders of world

religions in that he actually claimed to be God (Jn.10:30). He spoke with great clarity about who he was and left people in no doubt as to his divine nature. Steve Kumar helpfully provides us with a summary of the claims that Jesus made about himself[51]. He states that Jesus claimed to:

- forgive sin – see Matthew 9:1-8
- judge the world – John 5:27, 30
- give eternal life – John 3:16
- be sinless – John 8:46
- be the object of faith – John 8:24
- answer prayer – John 14:13
- be worthy of worship – Matthew 14:33
- be the truth – John 14:6
- have all authority – Matthew 28:18
- be one in essence with God – John 10:30

This list is truly remarkable and by its very nature it forces us to make a choice about who Jesus is. Either we dismiss him as some sort of seriously deluded person, or we take his claims seriously. C.S. Lewis stated that when you think of the enormity of Jesus' claims, he was either, 'a megalomaniac compared with whom Hitler was the most sane and humble of men' or 'a complete lunatic suffering from that form of delusion which undermines the whole mind of man, or he was indeed God'[52]. What we cannot do is just sit on the fence, because these claims are simply too extraordinary to allow for that. Moreover, Ramachandra points out that if Jesus did not actually believe his own claims, then we would have no grounds for seeing him as a moral exemplar for the rest of us[53]. And if we hesitate to acknowledge the truth of his claims then our only choice is to dismiss him as a liar and charlatan, and thus make the accusation that the whole edifice of Christianity is built on a gigantic hoax inspired by a self-deceived fool.

Again his claims make him unique among all the founders of world religions, for none has claimed such a remarkable list of qualities.

Rose from the dead

Lastly, Jesus is unique among the founders of world religions because he rose from the dead. The resurrection is without question the greatest miracle associated with the life of Christ. It is remarkable not least for the fact that Jesus actually predicted his death and resurrection long before it ever happened (Matt. 16:21). Like all other key events in the life of Jesus, the evidence for the resurrection is overwhelming. It rests on four facts, namely, that he was dead; that he was buried; that the tomb in which he was buried was subsequently found to be empty; and Christ's post-mortem appearances to his followers and to others. If these four facts can be established beyond all reasonable doubt, then it follows that the resurrection can be safely be accepted as a fact of history. We shall now look at each of the four in turn.

The death of Christ

The fact of the death of Jesus is not difficult to verify. After all, his executioners were professionals who knew exactly what they were doing and it was very much in their interests to ensure that their victims genuinely did die. Of all the crucifixions that took place in Palestine at the time of Jesus there is no record of anyone ever surviving this brutal form of capital punishment. We can also look back with the benefit of modern science and see from the historical description that we have been given of the crucifixion, that all the medical evidence for death was there and clearly apparent[54]. It is reasonable therefore to accept the death of Jesus as a fact.

The fact of his burial

The fact of the burial of Christ is equally easy to verify. Burial did of course commonly happen following death, but the burial of Jesus is particularly interesting because of its detail. We are told that Joseph of Arimathea, a wealthy and prominent member of the Sanhedrin, the Jewish parliament, went to Pilate the Roman governor, asked for the body of Jesus, and placed it in his own tomb. Jesus was viewed as a scandalous figure by the authorities of his day and there was real danger in being associated with him because of this. There is no way that a prominent figure like Joseph of Arimathea would or could have his name linked with these events if they did not actually happen. Had it just been a made-up story, it would have been exposed within days. This overt link with Joseph provides us with compelling evidence that the accounts of Jesus' burial were factual and that he was indeed buried.

Empty tomb

The third fact that provides the evidence for the resurrection relates to the empty tomb. This, too, can be readily verified historically. At the Feast of Pentecost, which took place 50 days after the resurrection, the disciples were in Jerusalem preaching to the Jewish Diaspora who had returned to the holy city for the festival. Their preaching was a huge success, with many Jews converting to Christianity. Needless to say, this greatly angered the Jewish religious leaders because, despite having got rid of Jesus, they were now faced with the threat of his disciples carrying on his ministry. They would love to have stopped this preaching and prove Christianity to be fraudulent.

At the heart of the message that the disciples were preaching was the claim that Jesus had risen from the dead. They were also preaching this message in the very city where Jesus had been buried. The solution, therefore, could not have been more simple for the Jewish religious leaders. In order to disprove Christianity, all they had to do was to produce the body of Jesus. If they did this then not even the most ardent follower of Christ would be able to claim that he had risen from the dead. But they did not do this; indeed they could not, for they knew full well that no body was in the tomb; it was completely empty[55].

Appearances

The final verification of the resurrection of Christ is the post-resurrection appearances of Jesus. These are most interesting because Jesus did not appear just once, but several times, and to many kinds of people in different places. He appeared to individuals, to small groups and, on one occasion, to a gathering of more than five hundred people. Some critics have tried to suggest that these appearances were a form of hallucination, but Little counters this claim in the following way:

> Hallucinations occur generally in people who tend to be vividly imaginative and of a nervous makeup. But the appearances of Christ were to all sorts of people. True, some were sensitive, but there were also hardened fishermen like Peter and others of various dispositions. Hallucinations are known to be extremely subjective and individual. For this reason, no two people have the same experience. In the case of the resurrection, Christ appeared not just to individuals but to groups, including one with more than five hundred people. Paul said more than half of these people were still alive and could tell about the events (1 Corinthians 15). Hallucinations usually occur only at particular times and places, and they are associated with the events fancied. However, these appearances occurred both indoors and outdoors, in the morning, afternoon and evening. In general, psychic experiences occur over a long period of time and with some regularity. These appearances, however, happened over a period of forty days and then stopped abruptly. No one said they happened ever again[56].

It is also worth noting the sheer physicality of these appearances with Jesus inviting Thomas to touch him (Jn.20:26-31) and later eating with his disciples by the seashore (Jn.21:1-23). This unquestionably rules out the possibility of these appearances being hallucinations. Many of these people later died for their belief in Jesus and his resurrection. Their martyrdoms provide further proof of the fact that they knew they had truly encountered Jesus after his resurrection.

Jesus' return from death undoubtedly makes him unique, for no other religious founder has died and then come back to life to be with his followers. Muhammad is dead, as is the Buddha and Krishna. Their followers do not dispute this fact and cannot because there is no evidence to suggest otherwise. Only Jesus is alive today. God raised him from the dead, after he had procured salvation for the world by his death on the cross.

So who has got it right?

We return now to the question that was asked earlier on. Why should we choose Christianity rather than any other world faith? In answering this question we need to reflect on the words of Jesus in John 14:6 where he said, 'I am the way and the truth and the life. No-one comes to the Father except through me'. This was an exclusive claim which denies that any other religion leads to God. Jesus does not give us any options here and he certainly does not allow for a religiously pluralistic response. He clearly states that we are either for him or against him and that there can be no other competitor for our affections. He exclusively claims to be the only way to God. This begs the question can we trust him? Why should we trust him over any other religious founder? The reason is obvious: the evidence clearly points to the fact that he is unique. He is the One we follow.

Chapter 7
Thinking about the New Europeans

Today's generation of European Christians face a challenge the like of which no previous generation has had to face. This challenge comes as a result of the increasingly multi-ethnic nature of contemporary European life. Generations of Christians in the past have had to face the challenges caused by medieval, enlightenment and even emergent thinking, but never before have Christians had to face the challenge of so many different faiths right on their doorstep.

Of course, Europe has always played host to peoples of other cultures and other faith systems. To some extent at least, there has always been a cultural and ethnic mix. But the scale to which ethnic diversity has increased in Europe in the past few decades is unprecedented. The primary reason for this increased diversity is that of immigration. In many European countries immigration is a hot issue, indeed in a recent British general election it featured greatly in the campaign with all the main parties promising a tough policy on immigration. Behind the rhetoric and posturing, however, is a complex issue that needs careful thought.

Immigration in Europe is on the increase (especially in

western European countries). It will also continue steadily for some time to come and for one very good reason – demographic change. This demographic change is not being brought about by war, technology or even a natural catastrophe, rather it is being brought about simply because people in Europe are not producing enough children. This has primarily to do with a change in cultural values, although advances in medical science have played a key part.

The sustainability of a population is dependant on either children being born, or on immigration. Most demographers think that for an average western country where life expectancy is high, there needs to be a birth rate of 2.1 children per woman to sustain present levels of population[57]. This however is not being sustained anywhere within Europe (with the exception of Albania) and is thus putting huge demographic pressures on the continent. Europe is not alone in this regard for the same is true of countries such as Japan and Australia. It is, however, as significant a problem in Europe as it is anywhere.

There are a number of reasons why this 'demographic meltdown' is occurring. These are strongly linked to European cultural values:

- Firstly there is the separation of sexual activity from childbearing. In the main, Europeans perceive sexual activity to be recreational as opposed to an activity which is also purposefully procreational.
- Secondly there is the widespread use and acceptability of contraception.
- Thirdly there is the phenomenon of career women either to fulfil feminist expectations or to enable couples to enjoy a higher standard of living. Because more women

are focussed on a career, there are fewer women whose major focus is having children.

- Fourthly, the prolonged educational experience which is widely available throughout much of Europe means that couples get married later in life. In general, the later a couple gets married the fewer children they will have.
- Fifthly there is widespread abortion. Put bluntly, the population of Europe has been reduced by millions since the 1960's due to abortions.

However, the decrease in population is only one side of the coin. Another problem is that people in virtually every European country are living longer. The result is that the ratio of people who are of working age is decreasing relative to those who are retired. For example when Bismarck introduced a retirement age of 65 into Germany, the life expectancy at the time was 45. Clearly things are very different now. Life expectancy in Germany is almost 80 and so the percentage of people within the German population who are retired is significantly higher. To have a high proportion of retired people in a country's population will eventually put pressures on the economy since those who are not working do not contribute to the productivity and wealth of that country. Ultimately this situation is unsustainable and in the long term many European nations will not be able to support their pensioners without radical change[58].

All this might seem a little alarmist, but consider the following:

Germany has a birth rate of only 1.4 children per woman. This gives them just a 60% population replenishment rate. Consequently if Germany does not let in any more immigrants, their present population of 82 million will fall to 38.5 million by 2100.

In the UK the birthrate is 1.69 births per woman. This means that without immigration the population will fall from 60 million to 30 million over the next 150 years.

Italy has a birth rate of only 1.19 births per woman, and Spain of only 1.07 births per woman. Clearly the crisis in these countries is even greater.

An EU report in 2002 stated that in order for Europe to maintain its present population, it would need to import 1.58 million immigrants per year until 2050 (a total of 75 million immigrants).

If the former Soviet Union were to be included in Europe it would have a population of 728 million. At present levels of decline, with no immigration the population would fall to 207 million by 2100.

Europe is often compared to the USA, and when this is done in relation to their relative birth rates it makes for fascinating reading. The USA has a birth rate of 2.1 births per woman, exactly the rate necessary for population replacement. Undoubtedly this is because the USA, unlike Europe, still maintains traditional values due to its strong religious heritage. The link between values and birth rates can be seen when comparing different parts of the USA. In Vermont, which is predominantly white, middle class, liberal, secular and European, the birth rate is only 1.57 births per woman – whereas in Utah which is deeply religious due to the presence of the Mormon Church, it is a very healthy 2.71 births per woman.

Needless to say, European governments will not allow this stark decline to occur. It cannot happen for it would be economically suicidal, not to mention socially, politically and militarily weakening. But as European birth rates are unlikely to grow without a seismic change in her social ethic, the only way to replenish the population will be through mass immigration. Thus we come full circle to the issue of the New Europeans – an immigrant population that is steadily growing because of more immigration. It should also be noted that this immigrant population is also growing because the birth rates among immigrant populations are higher than among European populations as a whole.

The question that needs to be asked at this stage is who are these New Europeans? The simple answer to this question is that most of these New Europeans are people from the developing world and most come from a non-Christian religious background, primarily Islamic. This clearly presents the Church with an enormous challenge to which it must rise.

Muslim Europe

The challenge can best be understood if we think about the emergence of Islam within Europe. If current trends continue, it is highly possible that by 2100 the Muslim population in some European countries could be as high as 40% [59]. Muslims could become the largest and most powerful interest group in Europe, significantly outnumbering evangelical Christians. That is not to say that the Muslim population of Europe will be a unified whole. Today's European Muslims come from a variety of backgrounds and cultures. Most British Muslims are Bangladeshi or Pakistani, whereas most French Muslims are North African. Germany's Muslims come from Turkey and Holland's Muslims from Indonesia. Despite this variety, Muslims are and will continue to make their presence felt throughout Europe.

Beginning to Witness

Given the enormous new challenge that the New Europeans bring to the continent, we need to give serious consideration as to how to reach them for Christ. One of the problems we will face is that many of these 'ethnic' communities are not well integrated into mainstream European life. In many cases they live in their own areas, continue their own culture and become 'ghettoised'. Sometimes the only way to reach them is to become part of their community and earn the right to speak, which is a lengthy process. Of course once we have earned the right to speak, the question remains, what do we actually say to them?

The Right Approach

Perhaps the starting point for improving our witness should simply be in the way that we approach people from other religions. Often Christians feel threatened by people from other faiths. In part this is fear of the unknown, but it is also a fear of the negative images many Christians have in their minds about other religions. Most of us have looked at our TV screens in horror as we have witnessed the atrocities of the Iraqi insurgency. Perhaps we recall news reports that described the brutality of Hindu or Sikh militants, or we reflect on some of the terrible martyrdoms in the past few years when Christians died at the hands of people from other world faiths. All of these images are of course real, as is the demonic power behind these incidents, but it is not the full story.

The reality is that although there are radicalised elements in all world religions, it is also true to say that the majority of the world's religious people are ordinary humans like us who are struggling to find their way in life[60]. They all struggle to do good while being tempted to sin. Just like us they get sick and become lonely, they feel fear and their lives are often characterised by disappointment. They are human with all the needs that human beings have, and they need our prayers and compassion.

If we approach them with this attitude we will find that they respond to love and friendship. Whatever culture or religious background a person comes from, friendship will be a valuable commodity. If we set out to be a friend, barriers will be broken down. Part of friendship will involve opening up our homes and being hospitable. In many developing world cultures, hospitality is very important. People offer food as an expression of respect and community obligation. By comparison many westerners are thought to be somewhat unfriendly and rude. We need to give careful thought to this important cultural difference. A Christian who is kind, practical and neighbourly will ultimately earn the trust of his Muslim or Hindu neighbour.

Another thing that we need to do is live a godly life in front of them. Of course this goes without saying, but often we forget very practical issues like this. In reality whenever we tell someone that we are Christians, they begin to scrutinise us to see if what we claim to believe makes any appreciable difference in our lives. This is where the rubber hits the road. Many Muslim and Hindu immigrants in Europe have already become appalled by the lack of morality they see. They believe Europeans, and westerners in general, lack sexual restraint, are disobedient to parents, are foul-mouthed and abuse alcohol. Of course this is true to a very great extent. The problem is that they also see Europe as a Christian continent, even though as we have already observed, this is patently not true. We need to live our lives in such a way that they can actually see the difference between true believers and those who are just nominally Christian. If they can see how Christianity is really lived out then they will be impressed and much more willing to listen.

From a practical point of view it is also important to be able to talk to someone from another religion one to one. If they are in the presence of others who share the same faith they are likely to be looking over their shoulder to make sure they do not say anything that is inappropriate or unacceptable in any way to their religious beliefs. We should never underestimate the ghettoised mentality of ethnic communities who feel naturally suspicious of any attempt to evangelise. Therefore it is useful, whenever possible, to talk with a Muslim or Hindu when he or she is alone and therefore not threatened by their perceived responsibilities towards their own people and faith system.

One last thing we must remember in reaching out to someone who comes from a completely different religious tradition is that we will need to be prepared for a long-term commitment. Such an enquirer will have a great deal to unlearn before they are able to receive the truth of the Christian faith. This will take time and require great patience. We need to remember that all the other world faiths are distinctly different from Christianity and therefore areas of agreement are limited, and even within those there are significant misunderstandings. The issue is further complicated by the fact that most religions do not only embody a set of doctrine, but an entire culture and way of life as well. Such is the diversity that we essentially need to explain an entire new worldview before the person and work of Christ can be properly understood. This requires that, little by little, we build up a picture of the Gospel and this is a process that simply cannot be rushed.

What do I say?

Having thought about our approach we now turn to the issue of what we say. It is difficult to be specific here because every religion is unique, as is every individual worshipper. There is therefore no one standard approach that works. What we can do, however, is reflect on some of the bases that need to be covered if our evangelism is to be successful.

Firstly, it can be helpful to state that Christianity is not a western religion because in the minds of our listeners there is often a connection between a geographical/political region and faith. If a person is Turkish or Arabian he must be a Muslim, if he is Indian he must be a Hindu, and if he is Western he must be Christian. This link between faith and geographical location is entirely wrong because God loves all and Christ died for all. However, those to whom we witness will still think of Christianity as a Western thing, and because they are culturally not Western, it is not a faith for them. We need to emphasise that Christianity did not originate in the West, that it is growing most quickly in the non-Western world and that the Christian God does not favour the British or the Americans over the Arabs or the Chinese.

Secondly, we need to stress that God can be known. This is a difficult thing to do especially when dealing with a religion that is as confused about God as in Hinduism, or one in which God is distant such as in Islam. Nevertheless the knowability of God is a vital component in our presentation because as human beings we have an innate spirituality, or as someone once put it, a God-shaped void in our lives. If a sincere religious person can come to the position where he realises that God does not have to remain distant but that He can be known personally, He will develop a hunger to know Him.

Thirdly, we need to stress a person's sinfulness. Again this can be difficult because not all religions believe in sin and divine judgment in the same way Christians do. Having said that, most people when pressed will admit that their lives are not as they should be, indeed they struggle even to attain the requirements of their own faith system. While we do this we should also pray that the Holy Spirit will prick their conscience so as to make them instinctively aware of their own fallenness. Once they become openly aware of their sinfulness the logic of divine judgment can be impressed upon them.

Fourthly, we need to focus on the Bible and in particular what it says about the person of Christ. While doing this we need to be careful not to openly criticise the founders of other faith systems. If we ridicule Muhammad or the Buddha we will lose a listening ear and gain nothing. Rather we need to keep to the discussion on the person of

Christ and his uniqueness. Some of the arguments used in the previous chapter will be useful here. If we demonstrate who Jesus is and why he had to come into the world then we will have achieved a great deal.

Finally, we need to deal with the issue of forgiveness and eternal life. Again this will be in conflict with some world religions, for example those that believe in reincarnation and karma. However the thought of receiving forgiveness now and being sure of heaven is a wonderful one. Christianity offers a hope that no other faith offers. If we have clearly spelt out the uniqueness of Christ and have been able to demonstrate how he fits into God's plan of salvation, then the hope of forgiveness and eternal life is one which they will be able to comprehend.

Of course, none of the things that I have suggested will guarantee a response from any of Europe's peoples. If only things were that simple evangelism would be an easy process. It is not! We need the power of the Holy Spirit working through us and convicting our listeners of their sin and the truth of the Gospel. Without the Holy Spirit's intervention no one will or can become a Christian. That means that above all else we should be prayerful in our approach to evangelism. But if we are open and walking in fellowship with the Lord, give thought to what we should say and then articulate our beliefs clearly, the Holy Spirit will be in a position to work on the seed that has been sown. In this way Europeans in each of these categories can be won for Jesus Christ.

Chapter 8
New Workers for a Europe Reborn

If anything should be clear by now it is that Europe is a challenging mission field. The complexity of European culture, created by a rich and dramatic history, means that anyone who commits themselves to evangelism within Europe will have an uphill struggle. Given this fact, it is important to ask questions about the kind of people who are suitable for working in a European context. In particular, we need to ask what qualities will be necessary in order for someone to work successfully as a missionary in Europe. A list of necessary qualities may, at first, seem intimidating. However, this should not be the case, rather this list should give anyone hoping to work in Europe something to aim for as they prepare for that task.

A strong spiritual life

The very first quality that any potential European missionary must have is a strong spiritual life. This may sound obvious, but it is a particularly important point to make, not least because many Christians assume that Europe, with its Christian heritage, will be a less spiritually challenging place to work than other parts of the world. This is far from the case.

European secularism has had a spiritually dampening effect on people. It has inoculated them against spiritual truth to the point where they are utterly apathetic. Missionaries and Christian workers can be affected by this. It is very stressful to work in an environment where profound spiritual apathy exists. It is discouraging inviting people to church repeatedly and then they never turn up. It is very hard to motivate yourself day after day for months on end when there seems to be so little fruit for your labour. If the missionary is to survive these rigours, especially in the long term, he will need to have a vibrant spiritual life.

Great patience

A second thing that is necessary when working in Europe is great patience. This is particularly true for missionaries who are involved in church-planting. The reality is that working in Europe involves a long-term commitment. This is not always true of other parts of the world. One missionary friend of mine who works in Zambia once told me that church-planting in the area where he works is a fairly easy thing. Indeed, he stated that if a missionary is not able to plant a church within five years, there must be something wrong either with him or his methods. This is because people in Zambia are spiritually responsive and live in a society where church-going is a norm.

Europe is quite the opposite. Some European mission

agencies estimate that a church-planting project could take 18 years to accomplish. This is a huge commitment and the work involved in reaching out to spiritually resistant Europeans is immensely difficult. Anyone wishing to work in Europe must be patient, work diligently, and wait upon God to produce a harvest.

A firm grasp of apologetics

A third quality needed to work in Europe is a firm grasp of apologetics. Europeans do not lack educational opportunities. They enjoy a high level of functional literacy as well as a very good university system. Europe as a whole has a rich intellectual heritage and has been on the cutting edge in the sciences and philosophy for centuries. There are, therefore, very few people within Europe who could be described as 'uneducated'.

In addition to this there is a general scepticism (perhaps even cynicism) with regard to Christianity. Europeans are well aware of the world around them and show an interest in and concern for world events. They know that Christianity has to compete in an ever more crowded marketplace of religious ideas and many are unconvinced that the Christian faith is any more important or true than any other world religion. Because of this, it is not uncommon when doing evangelism to find people who are able to argue persuasively against Christian belief and articulate their own worldview.

It is important, therefore, to be equipped to answer questions on a whole variety of issues. These might include some of the following:

- The evolution vs. creation debate
- The issue of religious pluralism
- Issues relating to ethics
- Life after death experiences
- The historical reliability of the Bible
- God as wish fulfilment
- The problem of suffering
- The deity of Christ
- The reality of sin and salvation
- Universalism
- The purpose of life

In my own evangelistic endeavours, I have found myself debating all of these issues with a whole variety of people. My overwhelming impression was that the people to whom I was witnessing were not just dredging up these questions for the sake of being argumentative, rather they had genuine questions and doubts and were looking for meaningful and satisfying answers.

Most people will not accept superficial and ill thought-out answers. Moreover many will feel patronised and will be 'turned off' the Christian message if it is delivered to them in such a way. It is necessary, therefore, to prepare ourselves in such a way that we are able to articulate the Christian faith intelligently and coherently. This will involve a serious study of the issues and the Biblical response as well as a sharpening of our communication skills. This preparation can be done in the context of a local church if it is well organised and there are competent people within the church who are able to deal with these issues in sufficient depth. However, in most churches this facility does not exist and so a period of training at Bible college would be very helpful. If this is not possible there are excellent short courses and good books available.

A deep Biblical and theological knowledge

Fourthly, missionaries working in Europe need to have a good knowledge of the Bible as well as a workable knowledge of theology. It is important to bear in mind that Europe is a continent in which many important theological debates have taken place and many new theologies have been spawned. Although it is true that most Europeans do not read the Bible, it is equally true that there is a general awareness of the Biblical storyline and the differences between the major strands of Christendom. Most Europeans are also aware of the non-Christian religious options that exist. People witnessing in Europe are, therefore, not speaking into a vacuum, but rather into an eclectic mix of religious ideas.

I can remember on one occasion being asked to explain why I did not pray to Mary. On another occasion I was asked why I did not go to Confession or celebrate All Saint's Day. I have also had to debate the issue of the authority of the Pope and the place of tradition in theology. In all of these situations it was important that I drew my response from Scripture. Only the authority of the Word of God is adequate to counter the misguided theology that prompted these questions.

I would stress once again that people who asked these questions were sincere and devout, they were seekers not cynics. Their intention is to serve God and to please Him and they genuinely believe that as they follow their religious practices they were doing just that. Anything less than a thoroughly biblical response, delivered with sincerity and compassion will simply not have any effect.

A general political and social awareness

In addition to the 'spiritual' qualities mentioned above, I believe it is also important for missionaries working in Europe to have a good general understanding of the political and social structure of Europe. Like many parts of the world, Europe has a rich and varied history. Many national traits in the component countries are explicable on the basis of history. Moreover many Europeans are proud of their history and accomplishments. They would understandably find it strange if someone who was working in their country did not understand at least something of its history.

Not only are Europeans proud of their own history, they also have an interest in what goes on in the world and pride themselves in their internationalism. In the past, Europe has played a significant role in world affairs and this continues to be the case. Most Europeans want their national institutions to interact with the world and many European charities busy themselves in some of the most deprived and dangerous places on the globe. It is therefore not unusual to find Europeans with strong opinions about places well beyond their borders. It would seem appropriate, therefore, that anyone working in Europe should have at least a rudimentary awareness of geopolitical events.

Friendship evangelism

A sixth quality which is needed, especially if the missionary is going to be involved in a ministry such as church-planting, is the ability to evangelise through friendship. It is a simple fact that most Europeans, especially those under the age of fifty, do not go to church. By complete contrast to North America, Latin America and parts of Africa, Europe is a continent where the Church wields very little influence. Even some of the Europeans who claim to be 'Christians' do not see church attendance as a necessary part of their religious practice.

Not only do most Europeans not go to church, they are also unresponsive to invitations to church. Church attendance is simply not a burning issue and it is something that cannot be coerced. This inevitably means that the key to working in most European countries is friendship evangelism. Prospective missionaries need to grasp the need to make friends in a natural way so that they can share their faith through friendship. Evangelism simply cannot take place without an audience, and the only way to get an audience is by befriending one. Developing skill in friendship evangelism will prove a great asset.

A flexible approach to Church life

A seventh quality which missionaries to Europe must possess is flexibility with regard to Church life. Life in Europe is very diverse. People living in large sprawling cities will have a very different experience of life to those living in the peaceful countryside. Likewise a successful and wealthy European business man living in the leafy suburbs will have very different expectations to those of an unemployed young person living in an area of urban deprivation. In addition there are also numerous sub-cultures which operate within European society. These include immigrant minorities who are often committed to a non-Christian religion, young people who are often disaffected, and the elderly who often struggle to cope with their rapidly changing environment.

Such diversity can require a varied approach to Church life. Not only might this involve using different church formats, it can also involve using different church models. For example, a model of church that has been used in a rural context where land is cheap and buildings easy to obtain, might not be appropriate in an urban area where the opposite is true. Likewise in a context where family and leisure time is rare and prized, the model of church might need to be altered so that people are not tied up extensively on a Sunday.

A willingness to work with national churches

It is always important to bear in mind when entering another country as a missionary, that there are churches already there. The goal of mission should be to build up a strong and confident indigenous church. Missionaries need to bear in mind that although they will one day return to their own countries, the national Christians are there to stay. Every effort must therefore be made to affirm national leadership.

This has significant practical implications when it comes

to missionary work in Europe. Missionaries coming into the situation should always be in contact with national church leaders and be prepared to listen to them and follow their guidance. Just as Europeans are well educated and proud of their heritage, so are European Christians. Any missionary who lacks humility or feels that he has all the answers to the problems faced by the European church will struggle to fit in or find acceptance. Likewise missionary organisations need to maintain an ongoing dialogue with national church leaders and see their work as complementary to and supportive of the work of the national church, not in competition to it. Ultimately if major decisions and direction do not come from national church leaders then the missionary or mission organisation will become isolated and lack impact.

A knowledge of comparative religion

The immigration issue has already been highlighted in Europe. Not only are there significant ethnic minorities living in virtually every European state, but these minorities are set to increase steadily over the next few decades. Most of the people within these minority communities will be adherents to non-Christian religions. Of these, the largest single group will be Muslims.

Today it is almost impossible to live in Europe and not come into contact with people from a non-Christian religion. This will continue to be the case, and therefore from a mission's perspective we need to be prepared for this. It will be necessary for any European missionary to have a working knowledge of all the major world faiths such as Islam, Hinduism and Buddhism. Missionaries will need to know how to respond to these faiths and be able to present a Biblical defence of the uniqueness of Christ. It will also be important to demonstrate a cultural sensitivity to people from ethnic minorities as they are often radicalised due to some of the racism which they have suffered.

Hermeneutics

One final quality which missionaries to Europe will need to possess is a familiarity with hermeneutics (the art of Biblical interpretation). Though last on the list, hermeneutics is arguably the most important subject that can be taught to missionaries hoping to work in Europe. Given the sophisticated nature of European life, and given that much of the Bible emerged in a non-European context, it is vital that workers in Europe have an understanding of how to contextualize and apply Scripture into living situations. In modern day Europe, the Bible is under siege from feminism, rationalism, liberalism and pluralism. Many theologians are trying to strip the Bible of its miraculous claims, make it more gender inclusive and dilute it so that other religions can be included in the promises of God.

The reality is that although the science of hermeneutics is discussed in depth in our universities, the result of these discussions can and does percolate down to street level. I have often found myself in discussion with non-Christians who assume that a God of love would never send a sincere Muslim or Hindu to a lost eternity. The assumption has already been made that the Bible should be interpreted in such a way as to negate this possibility. Likewise I have been asked why Paul 'hated' women so much and been told that the Bible must be read in a contemporary way so that women don't feel excluded. These pressures are constant in much of European Church life. Any missionaries hoping to bring the truth of God's Word into this context will need to be able to interpret Scripture accurately and in a relevant way, and that will necessitate an understanding of hermeneutics.

Chapter 9
Making the case for the evangelisation of Europe

If there is one thing that is clear by now it is that Europe is desperately in need of the Gospel. This is a continent with a wonderful Christian heritage and a great spiritual past. Europe has been the home of some of the greatest theologians, missionaries and Christian statesmen that the world has ever seen. It was the location for much of the ministry of the apostle Paul and became the centre of world Christianity. In recent centuries it was from Europe that the Christian faith spread to the Americas, Africa and the Far East. Europe was also the home of the Reformation which brought about a renewal within Christianity. Despite all of this, however, the Europe of today is a spiritually dark place and a continent in need of help.

A brief survey of the global picture would reveal a Church on the move. In Latin America, Africa and parts of the Far East the growth of Christianity over the past one hundred years has been absolutely staggering. Huge Church movements have grown from almost nothing and people have been ushered into the family of God in their droves. For all of this we as Christians should be profoundly thankful and rejoice in the way that God is clearly pouring out His Spirit. Amid all these celebrations, however, we need to reflect on the fact that in Europe, Christianity is shrinking rather than growing and secularism appears to have a greater hold on people than the Christian faith. Europe has become a post-Christian society and the spiritual challenge of this continent is arguably greater now than at any time in its history.

There is an argument that says that we should go where the Spirit is at work. Clearly the Holy Spirit is at work in Africa, Latin America and parts of the Far East. From a strategic point of view it would, therefore, make sense to put our resources into these areas where there will clearly be fruit for our labours. Certainly this kind of thinking has merit. It does make sense to work where the harvest is plentiful and to invest in something that readily produces dividends. However, if the availability of rich pickings was to be the only criteria by which strategic mission decisions were made then a great many people throughout the world would be condemned to live without Christ or the possibility of hearing about him. Given this I want to briefly outline some of the reasons why the evangelisation of Europe should remain one of the great priorities of the Church today and why we should continue to send missionaries to this continent.

Our first reason for focussing our efforts on Europe is that it remains a spiritually barren place. Whether the work in a particular place is easy or hard, whether people are responsive to the Gospel or not, the reality of people's spiritual need should be motivation enough for us. The truth about Europe is that more than 650 million of its inhabitants have no personal relationship with Christ and therefore, as far as any human can judge, are destined to go to hell for all eternity. This is a terrible truth to reflect on and I feel a real sense of foreboding as I write these words with trembling hands. But truth it is and we need to feel a sense of alarm for the spiritual plight of these lost people. Europe desperately needs the Gospel today and, given the fact that Christianity in the continent has been declining exponentially for the past one hundred years, the need could hardly be overstated.

A second reason for focussing on Europe is that what remains of Christendom within the continent shows little sign of being a source of spiritual help. Both the Roman Catholic and Orthodox Churches claim large numbers of communicants in Europe, however the reality is very different. Nominalism is on the increase and many of these communicants either disagree with much of what their tradition teaches or simply do not care enough to abide by it. Pope John Paul II summed up the situation well when stating that the Catholic Church needs to evangelise those people who had already been baptised. What is more, even if communicants are faithful to their Church traditions, the theological position of both Churches masks the simplicity of the Gospel and makes it difficult for people to find the truth or engage in a meaningful relationship with God.

A third reason for focussing our efforts on Europe is the serious global implication of not doing so. Europe still has a role to play on the world stage. It remains an economic and military powerhouse and the largest free trading block in the world. But it is also a continent of ideas, many of which have been exported to the rest of the world. It is logical to assume, therefore, that if Europe does not become Christianised once more, then European secularism might also leave European shores and spread to the rest of the world.

A fourth reason for focussing on Europe as a mission field is that the Church in Europe, if invigorated, will have much to offer the rest of the world. Europe is a continent that enjoys increasing prosperity, political stability and an unparalleled education system. The sad aspects of its colonial past notwithstanding, it has strong links with every corner of the globe. The church in Europe, though small, has benefited from 400 years of theological reflection since the Reformation. It does not require great imagination to see how these factors make Europe a great potential launch pad for further missionary endeavour if the Church were to experience renewal.

Fifthly, we should focus on Europe because it is a place where peoples from other religions can be reached in safety and in an environment where they may be free from the influences of family and society in a way they would not be if they were still in their homelands. I have a friend who is a missionary to Turks, but he has never been to Turkey. He witnesses to Turkish peoples in the city of Berlin. Another friend is involved in a project to establish a Kurdish Church in UK, who would never be able to go into Kurdish homelands in Iraq or Iran because of the security problem and political restrictions, but has complete freedom to share the Gospel with Kurds and can do so in safety.

The world is coming to Europe because of immigration. That means that the religions of the world are coming to Europe. It seems to me that in the sovereign will of God He is providing an environment within which the Church can take action and bring the Gospel to a lost people without the risks which would be involved if they lived in their country of origin. We must rejoice that many are coming to faith. For example it is estimated that in recent years some 2,000 Muslims in France have become Christians and joined a church. As well as rejoicing we should exploit this wonderful opportunity to the full.

From here on

I hope that you have found this book to be a useful guide to Europe and its spiritual needs. This book was never meant to discourage, but to challenge and to give us a real burden for this needy part of the world. Please pray for Europe and ask God what part you can play in reaching the 'Four Europes' for Christ. You might benefit from reading some other works which deal with some of the issues raised in this book.

A Primer on Postmodernism	Stanley Grenz	Eerdmans
And is it True	S. McQuoid & A. Noble	Authentic
Darwin on Trial	Phillip Johnson	IVP
Dissonant Voices	Harold Netland	Eerdmans
Europe Reborn	Ruth Marsh	Marc
Jesus among other Gods	Ravi Zacharias	Word
Operation World	Patrick Johnstone	Authentic
Scaling the Secular City	JP Moreland	Baker
The Case for Faith	Lee Strobel	Zondervan
The Uniqueness of Jesus	Chris Wright	Monarch

APPENDIX A

What the Reformation did for us.

The Reformation was a movement which began in the north of Europe at roughly the same time as the Renaissance was beginning in the south of Europe. Both movements were a response to the religious and secular abuses which occurred in the aftermath of the Middle Ages. The Roman Catholic Church had elevated itself in stature to the point where its authority was considered to be equal to, or greater than, that of the Bible and salvation had become something that people had to work for or merit. The Renaissance responded by making man an autonomous being and the centre of all things, while the Reformation responded by returning to scripture.

One of the key forerunners to the Reformation was John Wycliffe (1320-1384) who emphasised the Bible's supreme authority and produced an English translation which had significance throughout Europe. On the 13th October 1517 Martin Luther nailed his Ninety-five Theses to the church door in Wittenberg and thus the Reformation formally began. To put things in their historical context, this was just two years before the death of Leonardo da Vinci. Other reformers joined the foray and soon many Protestant churches began to form throughout Europe. By 1536 John Calvin had written his *Institutes of Christian Religion*, a key text for Reformation thinkers, thus signalling that the movement had reached maturity and was here to stay.

The Reformation brought a renewed spiritual zeal to much of Europe and provided Christians with an alternative to the Roman Catholic Church. Summing up the contribution that the Reformation made to religious life and thought is not easy, as it was a diverse movement, often characterised by furious debate between different reformers. However, significant developments took place on a number of fronts and these can easily be identified. Firstly, the Reformation produced a more Biblical doctrine of the Fall, one in which human beings were seen as utterly tainted by sin and unable to deal with this problem in their own strength. Secondly, the Bible was given its rightful place as the supreme authority in matters of faith and practice, with the church being under its authority. Thirdly, Christ was recognised as the only mediator between God and man, and the only one who could offer forgiveness and salvation. Lastly, the Reformation recaptured the doctrine of the priesthood of all believers. This meant that an individual believer could approach God directly by faith as a result of the finished work of Christ and not have to approach God via the institution of the church.

APPENDIX B

What is an Evangelical?

Within Christendom there are four broad groupings which could be labelled as Roman Catholic, Orthodox, Non-evangelical Protestant and Evangelical. Each of these groups is committed to a basic doctrinal position which includes an understanding of God as Trinity and the need for man to worship God. Evangelicals, however, are distinct from the other groupings in at least three ways.

Firstly, Evangelicals emphasise a definite personal conversion. They do not believe that someone becomes a Christian merely because he or she has grown up in a Christian country or family. Rather, each individual stands before God as a sinner and needs to be 'born-again' by having a personal conversion experience. Secondly, Evangelicals see the Bible as being the ultimate authority for faith and practice. It takes precedence over the church and human reason, both of which have to be brought under the authority of scripture and remain subject to it. Thirdly, Evangelicals deliberately focus on the person of Christ and his death on the cross. This remains at the heart of their theology and spiritual life.

Evangelicalism is not a denomination; rather it is a movement of like-minded individuals. Evangelicals can be found within the ranks of the various Protestant denominational families such as the Anglican, Lutheran, Presbyterian and Wesleyan, Baptist, Brethren and Pentecostal churches. In some cases Evangelicals form a minority within the denomination, while in others they are a majority. Sometimes an entire denomination can call itself evangelical because it requires an evangelical confession from all its members.

Evangelicals have traditionally had a strong commitment to evangelism and mission, consequently they can be found all over the world. They are the fastest growing branch of Christianity and in most countries are significantly more vibrant that any other form of Christian expression. They also have a keen sense of history and see themselves as inheriting the traditions of the early church. To Evangelicals, other expressions of Christianity are a departure from the New Testament principles which they treasure. They are characterised by a zealous abandonment to the will of God and a desire to live lives that are pleasing to Him.

END NOTES

1   Jonathan Hill, *The History of Christian Thought,* Lion 1998.

2   D.F. Wells, *No Place for Truth*, Eerdmans 1993 p.259-260.

3   S. Grenz, *A Primer on Post-modernism*, Eerdmans 1996 p.58.

4   D. Collinson, *Fifty Major Philosophers*, Routeledge 1987, p.57.

5   B. Russell, *A History of Western Philosophy*, Routeledge 1991, p.728.

6   Friedrich Nietzsche, *The Portable Nietzsche*, New York: Viking 1968, p.95.

7   Reaper-Smith, *A Brief Guide to Ideas*, p.168. Nietzsche felt that morals could not just be discovered, rather humans had to create them.

8   James Graff, *Time Magazine*, November 8 2004, p.36, 37

9   David Gow, *The Guardian*, October 28 2004, p.1

10   David Gow, The *Guardian*, October 28 2004, p.1

11   Patrick Johnstone, *Operation World*, Paternoster 2001.

12   This remains one of the most hotly disputed political issues in Turkey.

13   *Catechism of the Catholic Church*, p.26.

14   *Catechism of the Catholic Church*, p.27

15   *Catechism of the Catholic Church*, p.156.

16   *Catechism of the Catholic Church*, p.159.

17   *Catechism of the Catholic Church*, p.292.

18   By contrast Evangelical Christians believe in only two sacraments, those of Baptism and the Lord's Supper.

19   *Catechism of the Catholic Church*, p. 255.

20   *Catechism of the Catholic Church*, p.255.

21   *Catechism of the Catholic Church*, p.330.

22   *Catechism of the Catholic Church*, p.334.

23   *Catechism of the Catholic Church*p.346.

24   *Catechism of the Catholic Church*p.349.

25   *Catechism of the Catholic Church* p.351.

26   *Catechism of the Catholic Church* p.354.

27   Some further reading on these arguments will be presented at the end of the book.

28   It goes without saying that all of these traits as well as the four categories of people outlined can equally be seen in other parts of the world not least North America and Australia. However the focus of this book is on Europe.

29   Peter Hicks, *Truth, Can it be True*, Solway 1996, p.211.

30   It must be noted that this is also a limited definition because the word 'validated' is open to ambiguities, however it does function as a useful starting definition for the purposes of evangelism.

31   A useful exposition can be found in, Norman Geisler, *Baker Encyclopedia of Christian Apologetics*, Baker 1998, p.745.

32   Netland comments on this in his attack on John Hick, one of Europe's foremost pluralist thinkers, by saying, 'This is seen, for example, in the way in which Hick characteristically reinterprets troublesome exclusive

beliefs from various religions so as to avoid the problem of conflicting truth claims in religion' (*Religious Diversity and Religious Pluralism*, p.5).

33   Ravi Zacharias, *Jesus Among other Gods*, Word 2000, p.7.

34   Harold Netland, *Encountering Religious Pluralism: The Challenge to Christian Faith & Mission*, Apollos 2001, p.184.

35   Ibid., p.184.

36   Ibid., p.182.

37   Harold Netland, *From Athens to Jerusalem, Religious Diversity and Religious Pluralism*, p.5

38   Ravi Zacharias, *Jesus among other Gods*, p.5.

39   Some translations use the words 'God Breathed', see also 2 Peter 1:21.

40   And the total number of biblical prophesies would run into hundreds.

41   This includes over 5,000 Greek manuscripts, 10,000 Latin Vulgate manuscripts and more than 9,000 other early versions (Josh McDowell, *The New Evidence that Demands a Verdict*, Thomas Nelson Publishers 1999, p.34).
     For an important discussion on the significance of these manuscripts note the work of Bruce Metzger in *The Text of the New Testament*, Chapter 2, Important Witnesses to the Text of the New Testament, Clarenden Press 1985, p.36-92.

42   We also have a manuscript of the bulk of the New Testament from 250 AD and one of the whole New Testament from 325 AD (Josh McDowell, *The New Evidence that Demands a Verdict*, p.38).

43   Geisler and Bocchino go as far as to claim that the New Testament is 99.9% free of substantial or consequential error (*Unshakable Foundations*, Bethany House 2001, p.258).

44   Donald Wiseman, cited in Steve Kumar, *Christianity for Sceptics*, John Hunt 2000, p.111.

45   F.F. Bruce, *The New Testament Documents: Are they Reliable?*, Eerdmans 1993, p.104.

46   F.F. Bruce, *Jesus and Christian Origins Outside the New Testament*, Hodder 1984, p55, 56.

47   Sir Frederic G. Kenyon, Our Bible and the Ancient Manuscripts, p.55.

48   Ravi Zacharias, Jesus among other Gods, p.40

49   These are taken from a longer list of reasons found in *Protestant Christian Evidences*, by Bernard Ramm, p.140-143.

50   Some might want to dispute this claim insisting that other founders like Mohammed performed miracles. However, the alleged miracles of Mohammed are neither of the calibre of Jesus' miracles, nor can they be tested. As Craig points out, they were not claimed by either Mohammed or the Koran, rather they are a later and unverifiable tradition (Lee Strobel, *The Case for Faith*, Zondervan 2000, p.70,71).

51   Steve Kumar, Christianity for Skeptics, p.89-94.

52   C.S. Lewis, *God in the Dock*, Font 1987, p.88.

53   Vinoth Ramachandra, Faiths in Conflict, p.109,110.

54 Josh McDowell, The New Evidence that Demands a Verdict, p.224.

55 William Lane Craig provides a very compelling defense of the resurrection citing both the historical reliability of the texts and the individual components of the case (*Apologetics: An Introduction*, Moody 1984, p.167-206). With regard to the disciples preaching he notes how the early Christians suffered a most terrible persecution with many dying painful deaths. He then states, 'It is equally clear that it was for a miraculous story that these Christians were suffering' (p.176). This absolute commitment can only be explicable if they genuinely were convinced that the tomb was empty.

56 Paul E. Little, *Know Why You Believe*, IVP 2000, p.54.

57 This and other statistics mentioned in this chapter come from, *Why the West Hates the Rest*, by Meic Pearse, p.152-178.

58 Interestingly Time Magazine reports that Western governments have tried to combat the crisis with pension and labor reform but have shied away from urging people to have more babies (November 2004, p.44).

59 Already there are 3 million Muslims in Germany, 2 million in France, 1 million in the UK and perhaps 750,000 in Italy. (Philip Jenkins, *The Next Christendom*, Oxford 2002, p.97).

60 We have to recognize that there are radical elements in Christianity who twist the scriptures. This is distinct from the fundamental evil found in some other religious philosophies.